SustainABLE

How to find success as a sustainability professional
in a rapidly changing world

to John

hope you enjoy the
book !

Virginia

VIRGINIA CINQUEMANI

Foreword by Jerry Yudelson, "The Godfather of Green"

"Whether you think you can or you think you can't...you're right"
-Henry Ford

To my beautiful family – you give me strength

Virginia Cinquemani

SustainABLE: How To Find Success

as a Sustainability Professional in a Rapidly Changing World

© 2020, Virginia Cinquemani

ISBN: 9781674710419

Imprint: Independently published

www.thegreengorilla.co.uk

Illustrations and Back Cover Photography: Virginia Cinquemani

Summary

Acknowledgements

Writing a book is not easy-peasy.

Especially if you want to write in English and English is your second language.

If you haven't done it before - without a publishing house cleaning up after you.

And if you have a young family, a business, school runs, and Nativity plays to attend to.

So this book is much credit to all the people who supported me in this process. Without these amazing human beings, acknowledged here in no particular order, this book wouldn't have been possible.

My heart is overflowing with gratitude to you all.

- The nutty teacher that inspired my career in sustainability - Mario Martelli

- My lovely book coach - Deborah Ager

- My first two amazing clients - Elisabetta Li Destri Nicosia and Andromaque Simon

- The witty and knowledgeable Jerry Yudelson, "The Godfather of Green", author of the foreword and insightful expert reviewer

- The generous and supportive expert reviewers - Sune Nightingale, Stephanie Zumbrink, and Julia Craighill

- All the amazing sustainability professionals that feature in this book. You are such an inspiration! - Dave Cheshire, David Symons, Pantelis Levantis, Kartik Amrania, Tiziana Monterisi, Martin Brown, Martin Gettings, Nicola Hogan

- The incredible Green Gorilla coaches - Susan Heaton-Wright, Anthony McGee, and Anna Markovits - I've learned so much from you all! Thank you for inspiring much of this book and making Green Gorilla a reality

- My very patient proofreader - Cheyenne DeBorde

- My support network - Cristina Cucinella, Lois Barrett, Heidi Collocott and Edith Colomba - I'd be lost without you, sisters!

- My family - my children, Viola and Leonardo, and my partner, Gaetano - thank you, my loves, for bearing with me and with the many hours typing instead of attending to my mum/partner duties.

- Last, but not least, my wonderful readers - I appreciate your trust in my words and I wish you to become the best version of yourselves.

Foreword

In my late twenties, I was the project manager for an environmental con-
sulting firm in the San Francisco Bay area, preparing Environmental Impact
Reports (EIR) for various development projects, an early form of sustainability
reporting required by California law. I learned how to stand my ground on
the requirements for such reports, often through "trial by fire." Here's one
example.

One summer afternoon in 1974, I found myself sitting in an architect's conference room in San Jose. Sun streamed in though unshaded windows, the
room was stuffy, and a senior architect was yelling at me and my two colleagues. The meeting was decidedly unpleasant. We'd written an EIR on his
project, a medical office building proposed for construction on former tidal
wetlands near San Francisco Bay. He was angry because the draft of the report said, "Alternatives to the Proposed Project" (a section required by law
and regulation) should include reopening the wetlands to tidal action, letting it
function again as a saltwater marsh.

"That's not a reasonable option—no other project has to do this," he argued.
He wanted this alternative deleted from the report, but we wouldn't budge.

"It has to be in the report, or Marin County may reject it as not meeting
legal requirements," I replied. "If the report is incomplete, people may sue
your client and delay the project, so we need to keep it." After more heated
discussion, the architect relented and agreed that we can leave this section in
the EIR. This wasn't any garden-variety architect; he was well known – almost
famous - and his wife had a powerful position in local politics.

This project offered a chance to stake out a new claim: we shouldn't put de-
velopments in wetlands, a position which I strongly held personally. Instead, I
thought we should restore historical marshes, the most productive ecosystems

on Earth. Twenty years earlier, the Army Corps of Engineers straightened the adjacent creek and lined it with concrete, severely disturbing the marsh. Yet some wetlands remained. Our staff biologist had identified a listed endangered species living in the marsh, the red-bellied, saltwater harvest mouse, a small rodent that survived by eating marsh plants and drinking saltwater.

That little mouse turned the tide. After we convinced the architect, we added preserving the marsh (instead of building the project) as a reasonable alternative in our EIR. Both the architect and our team knew the local council would make the final decision, no matter what the report recommended.

The controversy alerted people in the area to the ongoing destruction of marsh habitats from filling in for development projects, a practice eventually halted around San Francisco Bay by the 1980s. After they watched a growing controversy over building on this marsh, the developers abandoned the project. Our work stopped this development, which pleased me immensely. The medical offices might have been a valuable project for the community, but they belonged somewhere else. The icing on the cake: later restored to full tidal flushing, the site is now a natural ecosystem protected as a local park.

Why am I relating this story? This incident happened a long time ago, but I still remember it as a defining moment. Speaking truth to power is not new, but it's often a challenge for young professionals, one that you must master to have a successful career. More importantly, to succeed in promoting the sustainability agenda, you must bring many tools to the task, not only your specialist training but also your personal skills of tact, persistence and advocacy.

I am so pleased that Virginia Cinquemani has written SustainABLE, bringing together what she's learned in two decades of work promoting sustainability. I could have used a guide like this when early in my professional career, instead of having to learn everything by trial and error and from what I could glean from more senior colleagues. More importantly, we know now that we don't have all the time in the world to move our economies and societies onto a more sustainable path into the future.

More than being zealous, we must become skilled and persistent in dealing with the worlds of commerce and government as we find them, not as we wish them to be.

When I first became an advocate for the U.S. Green Building Council's LEED certification system about twenty years ago, one thing that helped me was the ability to see the problem from many sides. In particular, I had an MBA and I was able to see the business issues at play, as well as the technical issues. Over several years, I became expert at understanding and presenting the business case for green building.

I realised that while a business might spend $2.50 USD per square foot for energy, they were spending $25 to $50 per square foot for rent, and $250 to $500 per square foot for people! So, where did it make sense to pitch the benefits of a green building? At the people! Even though it's energy usage that generates carbon emissions, it's people that drive the profitability of a business. My pitch changed: instead of just saving energy, I emphasized that healthy working environments reduced staff turnover (i.e. voluntary departures) and led to greater productivity.

Moreover, I stressed to many audiences that having a strong commitment to sustainability would allow them to attract and retain the best employees. And, after all, it's people who drive the "top line" (revenue) in a business. In today's world, with a paucity of early and mid-career employees available to most businesses, getting and keeping people is critical for any business (or university, government agency, NGO, etc.)

With a renewed focus on their business dynamics, I was able to convince many business owners and institutions to take another look at the costs of green building and certification, to understand that these costs were minor compared to the potential benefits.

Of course, there are many stages to everyone's growth as a sustainability professional. First you have to master the hard skills – the technical material or enough of it to be credible – but from then on, it's the soft skills that matter, the personal and relationships skills that will make you first a team leader and later an industry leader.

With its multifaceted hues and textures, sustainability is the defining personal, social and political issue of our times. Your commitment to be the best possible sustainability advocate is vital to addressing this issue, so Virginia's presentation of varied methods for personal growth and clever approaches to delivering sustainability is so important.

Take her message to heart; use what she teaches and become in your own way and in your own sphere, an awesome Green Gorilla!

Jerry Yudelson, The Godfather of Green

December 2019

A Note to The Reader

"A large latte, please!"

Ruth[1] winked at me.

"This is my little treat when I go and see clients. It's on expenses."

She grabbed a teaspoon and stirred three sugars into the half-litre of milk and coffee she was holding in her hands.

I gulped my espresso whilst we walked briskly to the client's office, a typical London architectural studio. On the outside, it kept with the Victorian look of the area, whilst on the inside, it was a buzzing sequence of white double height spaces and glass.

We introduced ourselves to the design team, sat down, and Ruth promptly pulled out the BREEAM[2] manual from her bag.

It looked more like a dictionary, with its 400 pages of technical criteria to assess the sustainability of the building our client planned to build.

She ran through a brief introduction on what a BREEAM "bespoke assessment" meant. In part, it included helping them put together the specific assessment criteria for this building, which wasn't falling within any of the standard types that the framework featured.

---

1 Names in this chapter have been changed.

2 BRE Environmental Assessment Method. Is the first ever framework developed to assess the environmental soundness of buildings.

And then off she went, picking one credit at the time, looking at the plans, and telling the team how hard it was to score in the "Daylighting" issue, because of the ambitious combination of illumination levels and daylight factors.

They also needed the right type of recycled aggregates, which could only be deployed for high-grade uses, if they wanted to qualify for the credit.

And their selected materials needed to demonstrate a chain of custody, which extended back to the extraction and the way they were manufactured.

And so on and so forth, for an hour.

One of the designers was taking frantic notes; the others nodded, in pensive silence.

I was observing, new to all of this.

I have to admit: at the time, Ruth impressed me with her knowledge of the framework.

At the same time, I could read in the architects' eyes an increasing puzzlement and a mixture of not-so-positive thoughts, the loudest being:

"This BREEAM thing is a right pain where the sun doesn't shine."

I could tell they were obviously perplexed by the apparent randomness of some of the criteria. That was paired with apprehension about the amount of information they had to provide to demonstrate compliance - on top of their standard work.

But they didn't dare ask many questions.

Ruth seemed oblivious to all of this - more preoccupied with fitting all her talking points into the single hour we had allocated with the team.

At the end, as jolly as she was at the start of the meeting, Ruth closed the manual, thanked them for their time, and swiftly left the room. I trotted behind her.

"Mission accomplished," she declared.

Ruth was very efficient. She managed to complete all of her projects on time and knew the BREEAM criteria inside out.

But did she create rapport with her clients?

Did she ask them what they wanted out of it? *Why* they wanted to undergo this process?

Did she reassure them about their concerns or tell them about the benefits of this course?

No.

In this case, the clients *needed* that assessment to be done, but they certainly didn't become advocates of **BREEAM**. They probably tried to avoid it like the plague in future projects.

Ruth was a sustainability professional with lots of confidence who failed to step into her clients' shoes.

Can you see yourself in Ruth?

Maybe you feel more like Lynn, an experienced sustainability consultant, who had lost her spark.

I've known Lynn for years through my work at BRE[3]. She's one of those sustainability consultants that delivers well project after project. Lynn requested a Skills Diagnostic call with me after one of my Green Gorilla Masterclass Programme introductory webinars.

I was sad to see her so deflated.

Lynn explained that she struggled to come to terms with the fact that, year after year, she was overtaken by younger, experienced colleagues, who somehow got promoted, whilst she stayed in the same position and pay as six years earlier. She was hardworking and knew her technical stuff, and yet, it seemed the management would not trust her in more senior positions. They didn't recognise her worth.

I asked whether she had *asked* for a promotion.

---

3 Building Research Establishment. Founded in 1921, BRE is one of the most prestigious and respected built-environment research institutions in the U.K. and beyond.

"No, I haven't. Isn't it obvious that I deserve one? But, you know, I'm part-time, and I think my boss doesn't like that; I feel that he thinks I don't work hard enough. And every time I ask him something, he ignores me anyway."

In recent research by Carnegie Mellon University's economics professor Linda Babcock, co-author of *Women Don't* Ask, it has emerged that men are four times more likely than women to ask for a raise — and when women do ask, they typically request 30% less than men.

Lynn's situation was typical. She didn't have the courage to ask, she had these conjectures in her mind that were stopping her, and she didn't have a strategy to move forward effectively.

In the meantime, she was increasingly unhappy and frustrated, and felt betrayed by the company she gave so much to in the previous six years.

Let's explore another example…

Gavin loves his job. He's a passionate ecologist, and loves carrying out wildlife surveys and environmental impact assessments in his native Scotland.

He graduated a couple of years ago and thoroughly enjoys the outdoor elements of his job. With that said, Gavin wanted to speak with me because, whilst he likes dealing with animals and plants, he struggles to engage with humans.

Every time he has to present his findings to a client, he feels lightheaded, his palms sweat, and his brain is foggier than the English countryside at 5am. For no apparent reason (because he is a skilled ecologist), Gavin looks, in his own words, incompetent and insecure. He stutters and his voice trembles.

It was clear to me that Gavin hadn't fully explored the self-limiting beliefs about his competence. Whilst a few nerves under stress are normal - and even useful to power the performance - Gavin hadn't developed a strategy to prevent his nerves from taking over when meeting new people or presenting.

Let's go for one more…

I met Miles at a breakfast event, which I organised to explore the key skills of environmental professionals.

He was an environmental advisor for an energy company. In his mid-30s, he seemed very self-assured, and had a great presence. However, when I asked the room what the number-one frustration of their profession was, Miles raised his hand and said: "I can't seem to make an impact."

We discussed his answer in more detail over coffee, and he explained: no matter what he said, his clients were in the vast majority of cases only interested in making a profit. It was hard for him to promote his values and ethics around sustainability, whilst also condoning his clients' ruthless point of view.

Does any of this sound familiar to you?

Have you ever found yourself in one of these situations? You dread going to work and making a presentation? You're torn between your sustainability beliefs and values, and a ruthless client? You're unable to create rapport with clients and wonder why they don't call back? You're frustrated by your own reaction to a work challenge – whether it's an argument, or your low pay compared to your level of expertise? You feel unable to step up and stand your ground?

No matter which applies to you, let me make it clear: you are not alone. Nowadays, thousands of individuals work in sustainability and environmental disciplines, and we all seem to share common traits to a certain extent.

A few years ago, I was working as the Head of Strategic Partnerships for the BRE's training department, and I was in charge of the membership scheme. I had over a thousand members, mostly BREEAM Assessors and Accredited Professionals. These qualified professionals guide their clients (developers, contractors, and design teams) through a process of evaluation and certification on the sustainability of buildings in line with the BREEAM (BRE Environmental Assessment Method) framework.

I was on the front line, hearing these professionals grumble about their clients on a daily basis. BRE, the body that, for over 100 years, has been at the forefront of the research on buildings in the U.K., was offering plenty of technical courses. However, these people were hungry for more direction on how to use their technical skills effectively. In particular, they needed to learn how to negotiate with their clients, explain the business case for sustainability to them, and influence design teams when they didn't have any authority over them.

At one point, we did a survey that asked consultants what other courses we could offer to better support them. The overwhelming response was that professionals needed help in more non-technical areas.

Yes, they needed technical knowledge, and **BREEAM** already offered a huge amount of information to digest and navigate through. However, it became apparent to me that technical knowledge was, in fact, not the final objective. It was only a starting point; the basic level they had to achieve in order to be successful in their profession. More social-based, communication skills were needed to make a real impact.

When it came to moving their clients towards **BREEAM** and, even more, towards sustainability in general, people didn't know where to start.

The real trouble began whenever a budget suddenly became tight, usually due to an unexpected situation in a project. Sustainability was immediately questioned and labelled as a "nice to have" rather than a "must have". The consultants had no idea how to incentivise their clients to still pursue the sustainability objectives of the project, in spite of the change in circumstances. For example, by stepping back and looking at their clients' core needs and wants, and prioritising those.

This is when I decided to explore ways of providing 'soft skills'-support to both **BREEAM** and other sustainability professionals who experienced the same issues. I wanted to offer courses so specific to this sector that they could resonate deeply and potentially change people's lives.

The world is full of courses; most of them give us information without changing how we work. I'd been in several management courses before. After a day of intense blah-blah, my head would spin and, at the same time, overflow and be empty. Nothing in my life would transform as a consequence of that course. Those courses weren't specific enough to address my own challenges in the sustainability sector, and, as a result, they didn't have a lasting impact on my life. I wanted to change that experience for my fellow sustainability professionals.

In 2018, I founded Green Gorilla as a training and coaching company to address the *soft skills* gap in the sustainability sector. In the process of developing my company, I often posed one question to my colleagues: what's the number-one frustration in your job?

I wanted to address their specific concerns. I wanted to respond to them in a way that no-one else had before.

At this point, dear reader, I invite you to ask yourself: What's the number-one frustration in your job? You may not work with environmental assessment tools, but your answers might be in line with those I received during my first survey:

"The hardest thing is getting clients to recognise the value of what they're asking for, from an environmental perspective, so they're less quick to dump it when the cost pressure comes on. Clients see the environment and sustainability as an extra cost or an unnecessary headache."

"Some clients are enthusiastic, and need to push sustainability hard in order to get the best tenants for their building; they want the most sustainable building they can get. So, they might apply the standards of BREEAM Outstanding/Excellent, LEED Platinum, WELL, etc. And they have the budget to do so.

Other clients, however - especially if they're cash-strapped and only fulfilling a need to meet planning requirements - will want the basic environmental assessment at the lowest possible cost. It's with these clients that BREEAM becomes 'challenging'; never mind trying to promote general sustainability on a project, which may be an even bigger challenge."

"Some clients are very cynical about spending lots of money on sustainability. They just don't feel the cost of it matches the benefits. When they find areas where they must implement sustainability, it's hard to maintain good cooperation."

Cooperation, perception of value, and trust (or the lack thereof) came back over and over again as key issues that sustainability professionals face with their clients.

Clients engage with sustainability because they have to, or as a marketing stunt. The ethical argument is a motivating factor for a very small percentage of clients – and that's often a façade placed in front of a business-related goal anyway.

For other professionals, their biggest frustration is confidence - especially in the boardroom during presentations and meetings. I suspect that, for many sustainability professionals, having strong ethical values as their main drivers means they also believe assertiveness equals imposing their own ideas (right or wrong) onto other people. This, in turn, feels unethical.

Some professionals know their technical stuff very well, but don't know how to communicate it for maximum impact.

Others have lost their spark. They encounter daily struggles in pushing sustainability, and may feel like the ' traffic wardens of an environmental assessment', as a fellow consultant once described it. This leaves them feeling empty and unsatisfied with their jobs.

So, this book focuses on helping you find new self-assurance by boosting your confidence in yourself, your knowledge, and your values. I want to provide you with a set of practical tools, so you can start making an impact like you've never managed to before. If you want to be listened to, be more confident, and start proudly offering the best possible service to your clients - every day...

Then read on.

How to Use This Book

Are you feeling frustrated in your current career? Or is everything okay, but you know you have more in you?

I'll show you how to reverse-engineer what's holding you back, so you can better unlock your real potential.

I wrote *SustainABLE* to support you in this transformative process, by sharing what I have learnt from my own and my fellow sustainability professionals' experiences, as well as from well-regarded leadership and management experts.

Part 1 looks at the background, explores the reasons why you might feel unfulfilled in your profession right now, and suggests practical ways to reignite your passion.

Part 2 explores the key skills you'll need in finding success as a sustainability professional, as well as how you can develop and refine them. At the end of each chapter, you can take some very practical *Action Steps* to enable you to practice my suggestions in real life.

You can download your *Action Steps Workbook* from **www.thegreengorilla. co.uk/sustainable-the-book.**

You'll notice that I've used many examples drawn from my experience in the built environment sector. This is where I acquired most of my know-how, but the general principles are applicable to any sector, as I learnt from speaking to professionals of other fields.

You can use this book as a reference manual, dipping in and out as you need it (you might have already mastered certain skills) or read it back-to-back. In any case, the most important task is applying the techniques that resonate with you in your job and life as often as you can.

Remember, new attitudes need to become habits first, and they will only become skills if you work at them consistently.

How I Was Saved By a Man That Set Fire to His Sink

As soon as I left school, I knew I wanted to be an architect. However, my passion and awe for the built environment was nearly killed by an impersonal system that didn't take the human factor into account.

A client with too much money and her six decadent bathrooms was the last straw. It gave me the final push I needed to seek a new path.

I got a dream job I didn't apply for. I learnt a great deal, but I knew my true calling was to step out on my own - to ignite positive change in other people. People like you.

Every weekday, I would depart from the train at the last stop - Palermo Centrale in Sicily - and take the 20-minute walk down the perfectly smooth (and slippery) stone pavement that led me to the School of Architecture. With my heart full of purpose, I loved strolling down that city-centre path, in constant awe of the decadent, neglected, and noble architecture. I could smell both mould and freshly-baked croissants wafting from the numerous coffee shops on those early mornings.

In the School of Architecture admission tests, I came fifth out of 500 successful candidates, and some 1,500 applicants overall. Initially, I read that as a sign from the universe that I was meant to be an architect.

I took my studies with the right balance of seriousness, fun, and curiosity. I obtained top marks in the majority of the 52 gruelling exams taken in five years before my final project and dissertation.

The year before graduation, I backpacked in Europe on an interrail ticket with my university friends. We were on a quest to see the best and most significant architecture of the continent with our own eyes. With my dad's Yashica film camera hanging heavy from my neck, I admired the masterpieces of big-name architects. Zaha Hadid, Frank Gehry, Le Corbusier, and Renzo Piano popped out of my university books and into reality in shapes, textures, colours, angles that took my breath away.

"I'll be like them," I told myself.

My purpose, though, wasn't to build my own cathedral in a desert (my ego wasn't big enough for that). Instead, I'd create spaces that would challenge the norm, fit around people like gloves, and make them happy about where they lived, worked, and played. I wanted to bring the outside *inside* in clever ways. I admired the creativity of the masters and felt surprised by the new, exciting feelings inspired in me by those places.

That same year, I had an architectural design teaching assistant who challenged the status quo often - and uniquely. For example, he would walk on (rather than *around)* the bonnet of cars that were badly parked on pavements, blocking the way for pedestrians - I'm sorry to say, a very common Sicilian scenario.

At home, he would clean his bathroom by setting the basin and WC on fire with pure alcohol and a lighter – after all, fire kills bacteria.

Mario Martelli was the first free-thinker I ever met, who could challenge with enthusiasm any existing state of affairs in the name of justice and common sense, never fearing judgement.

Mario's influence was key to my formative professional years, not in the least because he was the first to ever mention the word *"bio-architettura"* to my fellow colleagues and I: architecture that integrated with nature. Rather than negatively impacting it, it worked in tandem to power the building's functions in a gentle, respectful way. It's not the architecture of big statements but, rather, architecture that 'makes sense'.

My other lecturers would sit down and read from their notes, with no visual aids, and talk about how we should worship the masters of brutalist architecture - especially those who left concrete structures and mechanical systems exposed in their 'honest' language.

It was generally three hours of philosophical theories around the meaning of rational modern architecture... and the importance of Le Corbusier in our work as architects... and more "blah blah blah"'s that were so impractical.

By the end, it was so far from the human element that not even my two morning double-espressos could keep my eyes open.

In stark contrast, Mario jumped up and down the stage excitedly, using plenty of images and fascinating stories to deliver visionary lessons, during which he showed us those first buildings constructed in the middle of forests, featuring garden roofs, mud walls, and organic shapes. Light was a design element; the environmental performance of the buildings was key to their occupants' health and well-being. He would show us how wood, plants, and natural light created homes where people thrived; they weren't just cardboard shapes in a 3D artist impression.

After a full day of this, I would head back home from my classes. I used to live with my family in a large flat on the seventh floor of a badly constructed 1970s building in the outskirts of Palermo. In spite of the mild external temperatures, the flat was cold in wintertime with no heating, to the point that I would sometimes go to bed wearing a woolly hat and scarf. In the summer, the flat grew hot thanks to the lack of insulation and the metal, single-glazed windows. The cheap facing of the walls crumbled in areas. My home wasn't very different from the majority of dwellings in my city and, in fact, in many other parts of Italy.

As you can imagine, those incredible buildings I saw in Europe and in my teacher's lessons were a far cry from what I was used to. But they had a lasting impact on me.

Graduation day approached. It was a mad rush to finish everything on time, from writing the last words of my dissertation, to polishing the accompanying drawings (I felt very modern indeed, using 2D CAD for the first time in my university course, alongside hand-drawn perspectives). Finally, I slipped into my new black suit and red t-shirt (I wanted to look like a proper architect) and visited the School of Architecture to present my thesis to the university committee.

It went remarkably well, and five and a half years of hard work paid off. I received top marks and a mention - to the elation and relief of my whole family, who sat behind me in the faculty's conference room.

Then reality hit.

A week after graduation, I was in the U.K. with the intention of staying. I had never even visited the U.K. before, but the thought of dealing with a toxic mix of backwards mentality, mafia, bureaucracy, and possibly having to strike dodgy compromises in order to work in Sicily didn't appeal to me in the least. I was a young woman and wanted to work in construction, a sort of prized cow in the U.K. at that time, but even more so back home where, unfortunately, the construction industry was lightyears away from the British scenario.

I remember weeping when I heard that three of my best friends were graduating too and I wasn't there with them to celebrate. Instead, I was sweeping floors in a Chinese restaurant late at night. The kitchen staff couldn't or wouldn't learn my name, so they called me Italy Two – as opposed to Italy One, my fellow Italian colleague who arrived there before me. To be fair, I couldn't speak English either at that point. Only a 23-year-old can move to a country where she doesn't even know how to reply to *thank you*.

Nonetheless, after a year of learning basic English, working in coffee shops in the morning, and labouring in restaurants at night, I managed to get a job in a very small but well-respected architectural firm in South London. I personally brought my CV to all the architectural firms in my area hundreds of times, and showed up at this particular architect's door four times at least. I got him by exhaustion, I believe. But, I was desperate to move on with my life, follow my calling, and use my degree.

Work was hard. I was the only employee, alongside my boss and his wife, who would work on the admin side of things. I admired my boss, an old-school guy who possessed magnificent ego and creativity in equal measures; he was a generous, welcoming, and genuine person, but he wasn't the easiest human being to deal with.

He couldn't understand that I was trying to learn a method of building that was completely different from what I'd studied In Italy. On top of that, my architectural school had been 95% theory and 5% practice – thank you, Italian university. At the office, our creativity was often killed by an obtuse or capricious client with more money than sense; by an engineer, who would try to temper in my boss' ambition; or by the local authority, who wouldn't approve our projects unless they conformed to the dull planning rules.

I began to wonder whether Zaha Hadid was an alien, who just dropped the Vitra Fire Station from her spaceship whilst altogether bypassing the local planning officer.

A year in, I was beginning to feel uninspired. After much deliberation, I decided to go back to what actually sparked joy in my architectural studies. I applied for a part-time MSc course at Oxford Brookes University in Energy Efficient and Sustainable Building. I commuted two days a week to Oxford from South London, whilst working at the architectural studio for the other three days.

The course reignited that excitement and feeling of purpose I was craving so desperately, and reminded me of my nutty lecturer's classes in those undergrad years. It felt wonderful to be part of a community of like-minded people, and a field trip to the Findhorn Ecovillage in Scotland sealed the deal for me. I wanted to create buildings that moved people to live the best, most inspired lives they could; designs that would mirror their owners in a symbiotic way.

A few months into my Master's, I found a new job in another small studio that claimed they had sustainability as a core value - and they would pay me double what I earned at my old place.

I soon discovered that, for them, sustainability was no more than a marketing claim - and quite at the bottom of my (three) bosses' priorities. It was another disappointment, but I didn't want to give up at the beginning of this new adventure. Besides, I enjoyed my morning stroll through posh Chelsea, which felt a bit like being Pretty Woman without the budget.

The idiosyncrasies I found in my previous employment were exponentially bigger here, with less creativity, more frustration, worse stress, and constant worry around the new responsibilities I was given.

The straw that broke the camel's back was a job to refurbish six luxury bathrooms in a mansion in Chelsea. Our client was a strong-minded American lady, who obviously didn't trust us in the least. For the long meetings about the project, there were eight people around the table: one of my bosses and I; our client; the contractor and his assistant; two interior designers; and a personal advisor to our client.

All that, just to keep that same outdated design as before (flowery, fabric-upholstered walls, anyone?), just with new materials.

She wanted (and got in the end) a plastic tunnel that would take us from the front door, through the house, and to each bathroom. This prevented dust from settling on the other rooms. If you have seen E.T., you can picture this easily.

Six.

Flipping.

Bathrooms.

The lengthy discussions about where the toilet brushes should go, paired up with the sexist and patronising comments in the office and on-site, ended up being too much for me.

So that's when I decided to quit architecture for good and sent an email to BRE, asking how I could become a sustainability consultant. After all, BRE was the U.K. authority in sustainability in the built environment, so surely they knew how I could make the leap.

The reply back asked whether I had a CV that I could send through.

The next reply asked whether I wanted an interview. And that's how I got a job without even applying for it, working in the young and vibrant BRE technical team to help write the **BREEAM** guidance that we use today to assess sustainability in buildings.

I finally felt I was making a difference.

After nearly 12 great, mostly inspiring years there, I took a leap into the unknown and started Green Gorilla. I wanted to help fellow sustainability professionals feel more empowered via tailored, soft skills training and coaching.

I'm telling you my story for three reasons:

1. You are not alone. If you are a tree-hugger, be proud of it. My quest for purpose in my job led me to what I am today. It took me 15 years to get there, but I ended up where I wanted to be, and it feels good. It feels right. It feels like I'm doing what I am meant to be doing, and that I'm making a difference, in spite of daily hiccups.

As a sustainability professional, and as a human being in general, I realised that happiness at work depends on the gap between reality and our aspirations, values, and beliefs. The smaller the gap, the higher the sense of fulfilment and happiness.

In this book, I offer you ways to reduce that gap, bringing reality closer to your aspirations. You may not be able to completely change the world right now, but you can change the way you see and are seen by others. That will have a massive impact on your fulfilment and the difference you make in the long run.

2. *There will always be people less inspired than you, and that's okay.* Hopefully, through this book, you will work to own your inspiration, so that it refuels your passion and ability to infuse it with others. However, you'll need to accept that, sometimes, it's okay to move on. There are some people in the world for whom sustainability and the environment are not a concern, in spite of scientific evidence and obvious climate change events.

3. *You need to develop resilience.* The sustainability world can be tough, so the best way to achieve your goals is to keep pushing - despite setbacks. Whilst learning to walk, if a baby stopped getting up every time they fell, they'd never run. If I had kept working at a Chinese restaurant for 10 years, instead of spending every minute of my free time knocking at architectural firms' doors, or if I

stayed at my assistant architect job, feeling belittled and unfulfilled, I never would've started this profession. I wouldn't be where I am now, happily doing what I do, making my small but sure contribution to a better world.

I'm sure you've had your fair share of falling and getting up, so you can relate. However, if you're struggling where you are right now - if you think it's hard or impossible to be happy in your current situation - ask yourself:

Does the thought of becoming a successful sustainability professional feel right to you?

If it feels 'light in your heart', then just keep getting up. I bet you're closer to your goal than you think. All it takes is the right action steps.

Your grit - your passion and perseverance towards your long-term goal - will help you maintain the right path.

PART1

CHAPTER 1

Let's Start With You

You are working in sustainability because you believe in it.

Written like this, it sounds like a religion; and it sometimes is, judging from the animosity found in discussions with naysayers – sometimes even within our families. When I was told by a person I love deeply, *"You just sell hot air"*, my eyes nearly popped out of my head and I felt profoundly hurt.

Isn't it obvious that fossil fuels are polluting and adding unnecessary stress on the planet's delicate balance? Tipping it dangerously for generations to come, whilst renewable energy sources are not?

Isn't it obvious that clean is better than dirty? That reusing or recycling plastic, a material created using heaps of water and energy, is better than using it for 10 minutes and throwing it away, only to see it hanging around in the sea for the next 500 years, choking fish and turtles to death in the meantime?

Well, it turns out, no.

It isn't so obvious to many people.

You Have to Deal with Naysayers

Perhaps you are currently frustrated with your clients, who aren't showing any interest in what you're trying to do. They may have to demonstrate that their building is constructed using certain sustainability principles, because of planning consent or corporate responsibility, but they may not believe in it.

They may think sustainability is *hot air* - that it's a waste of time and money.

Perhaps you had grand plans - such as making this project you're advising on a unique example of circular economy - but your client said, *"No, we don't have the budget or the time for it, we'll just do the sustainability assessment,"* and you find yourself ticking boxes. *"Yes, yes, no, no, no…"*

We will get into the 'why' some people are not interested in sustainability later, but for now, let's focus on you a bit more.

If it's obvious to you that living and doing business sustainably is a matter of common sense - that, in fact, there isn't another viable way of living and doing business for you - then that means sustainability is a value for you.

Values are ingrained in us. Although they can shift slightly in life, they are something we deeply believe in, so they tend to compose a vital part of our being.

That also means your profession tends to be less of a job and more of a passion.

Do you find yourself picking up litter as you walk the dog in the park? Do you recycle your supermarket receipts? Do you ensure your computer is off every night and that people in your household switch off the lights when they leave a room? Perhaps you own an electric car or have a Tesla on your wishlist?

If you deeply believe in it, and it's also part of your private, everyday life, then it's something that resonates profoundly in you. When it's part of you, it's a vocation - and that's a good thing to reconnect to if you're feeling the struggle of a daily grind with sceptical clients and colleagues.

You Feel That You Are the Defender of Sustainability at Any Cost

At the moment, though, you might be struggling with something more personal. It's different than obnoxious clients, but it will kill your motivation all the same.

Perhaps you're one of those sustainability professionals that wears an armour to work every day. Like Don Quixote of La Mancha, YOU ignore the world as it is, ignore your clients' needs, and prefer to imagine that you're living out a knightly story. *"Yes! We need to save the world! We are the knights who will defeat our enemies and save the planet!"* But then you encounter your own windmills in the boardroom. They hit you hard. You don't know how to challenge them, so you collapse.

The Daily Grind and Nitty-Gritty Got the Best of You

Or perhaps you take the big picture for granted, to the point where you no longer feel responsibility for pulling others onto your Noah's Ark. Instead, you focus on the minute, technical details, such as the stress of the environmental impact assessments, appraisals, or certifications.

You Suffer From Impostor Syndrome

Or do you have a niggling doubt that you're not good enough? You want to change; to take ownership of your career, emotions, and behaviours; to *step up*... but, deep down, you don't think you have it in you. You are a technical person and an environmentalist. You may not see yourself as a leader (yet), or as a business person who can negotiate successfully, even about your paycheck.

You Gave Into Doom and Gloom

Or perhaps you walk into the world defeated. After all, knowing too much about the grim stories - climate crisis, ocean pollution, mass species extinction, ozone depletion - can be a curse. So, you lost faith in changing the world one project at a time, one client at a time.

You ask yourself: What's the point?

But it's not too late. It is possible to find your motivation again - to rediscover the fire that pushed you to choose this path, this career, this life, no matter how negative your circumstances or your own attitude looks right now.

How?

Let's explore the psychology behind certain characteristic behaviours of environmental professionals, and what we can do to change them.

Key Points to Remember

Feel free to use this space for jotting down notes on your personal takeaways from this section.

CHAPTER 2

The Psychology of Environmentalism

In this chapter, I'll cover some practical methods for reframing your anxiety (or the anxiety of people close to you), so you can better overcome it.

Human beings are part of a magnificent bigger picture. Did you know that we share 30% of our genetic code with fungi? Think about any structure and system in nature - for example, a tree. Its branches' pattern is very similar to the way our brain is wired. We breathe and we eat living things – even the vegans out there, who still eat living organisms. We need daylight and water just like any plant.

It's no surprise that incorporating elements of nature into the built environment has been demonstrated through research to reduce blood pressure levels, stress, and heart rates, whilst increasing productivity, creativity, and well-being. This is the concept at the roots of biophilic design.[4]

---

4 www.oliverheath.com

We are part of nature - we *are* nature. And the more we detach ourselves from it, the more we build bunkers of concrete and steel, the more we step further away from nature, the bigger our sense of isolation and uprooting.

Dramatic climate change, and the rapid transformation of the world around us at the hands of men, is instilling a condition in some people called *'solastalgia'* - a sense of loss that we experience when the environment as we know it is changing dramatically, so much that we don't recognise it anymore.[5]

In the minds of environmentalists, and sustainability professionals in general, this process is amplified. We are deeply conscious of our personal impact on the environment, because environmentalism is a value in our lives. Furthermore, we feel like Cassandra of Greek mythology, with our just warnings and concerns dismissed or disbelieved - to the catastrophic detriment of everyone.

Additionally, we might experience *cultural dissonance*, when we feel guilty of living a lifestyle accepted as 'normal' by society, but which we understand as unsustainable in the long-term. For example: flying two or three times a year, buying food wrapped in plastic in supermarkets, and shopping in high street clothes stores that have dubious ethical and environmental policies in producing their garments. Simple things, like going shopping or planning a holiday, become major guilt traps for sustainability professionals.

Add to this the social media comparison. It's not just teenagers who fall into that trap. My Instagram feed is full of 'green hearts', and although this nourishes my love for both sustainability and the sense of having found a tribe, I'll admit: when I came across the woman that can put five years' worth of waste in a glass jar, I felt a sense of unease and self-doubt. *"Why can't I? How does she do it?"*

So, I started scanning my own life for opportunities to bring down my waste impact. I planned weekly trips to my local, zero-waste shop for some of the groceries I needed, I subscribed to an organic veg-and-fruit-delivery scheme,

---

5 I first came across the psychology of environmentalism when I attended a webinar by Sam Hall, psychotherapist and sustainability consultant. He magisterially explained the issues and potential solutions to a very complex psychological phenomenon that can affect many environmental and sustainability professionals.

and then I thought: *"What about plum tomatoes? They come in a can. And oat milk? It comes in a Tetra Pack carton; that's not recyclable, is it?"*

You can see (and maybe you can relate with) how the behaviour of someone on social media created my anxiety. And, of course, social media often gives you the shinier side of people. I since realised that she recycles some of her waste; it's not that she doesn't produce any at all.

The reality is that the lives of environmental professionals can be a persistent conundrum. It cycles between heartbreak, because what we value is being destroyed before our very eyes; a feeling of helplessness, because time is running out to halt or prevent it; and even guilt, because we might be aware of certain solutions, but still inevitably be part of the problem.

> *"Living the examined life is a pain in the ass."*
> -Yvon Chouinard, Founder of Patagonia

This toxic mixture of feelings can lead to anxiety, bereavement, isolation, anger, and depression.

There are ways to come out of it, though.

You need to remember: there is always a choice - and, in this case, you can do something about it.

The key starting point is in being aware of those feelings, then choosing to act upon them in a deliberate way.

For example, we can *choose* to act differently when receiving bad news. It can be depressing, but it shouldn't lead to depression.

We are surrounded by doom and gloom. From the exceptionally hot summer of 2018 and the IPCC[6] report, which predicted we have only 10 years left - at the most - to address the climate crisis meaningfully, the media has increasingly picked negative environmental stories. They make emotions run high – and, thus, it sells better. The media particularly loved the report by the IPCC; how wonderfully apocalyptic was that?

---

6 Intergovernmental Panel on Climate Change

But how to respond to doom and gloom? And how to avoid doom and gloom infecting you?

Start by processing your negative emotions and accepting them as they are, instead of clinging to them. It takes some effort, but the result is that, para-doxically, emotions lose their power on us. *What you resist, persists,* so it pays to let the emotions exist for a short amount of time and observe them without judgement.

Try something like:

- Mindfulness.

- Formal meditation.

- Time off from media and general noise.

- Practising appreciation and gratitude.

- Journaling.

- Crafting.

- Spending time in nature.

- Physical exercise.

These practices can all help reduce anxiety levels and negativity. You may also want to consider counselling if you doubt your ability to shift the negative perspective by yourself.

Once you are aware of your emotions, you can channel them into action. Retaining hope and reframing the issues is important on a personal level for your mental health, and to become effective in your actions.

Certain elements are outside your sphere of control, and there is little you can do; make that sink in. You can't change the world single-handedly, but you can do and contribute a great deal towards it. You just need to prioritise where your efforts are focussed.

When thinking about environmental issues, if your dominant feelings are frustration and anger, you can turn them into passion. Because environmental issues are part of your value set, you can grow especially motivated to act for your kids or for the planet.

Whatever the feelings you're experiencing right now, if this transformative process doesn't lead to hedonistic happiness, it can certainly lead to a more fulfilling, renewed sense of meaning and purpose.

> *"The purpose of life is not to be happy. It is to be useful, to be honourable, to be compassionate, to have it make some difference that you have lived and lived well."*
> -Ralph Waldo Emerson, philosopher and poet

It's true: the issues humanity is facing are very real and interconnected, be they climate crisis, ocean plastic islands, biodiversity loss, hunger, war, or migrations. However, so are the possible solutions[7]. The IPCC's report encourages collaboration and collective action. At the time of writing, people have begun to rally together with Extinction Rebellion and similar initiatives around the world.

Take the student strikes, for example, headed by Greta Thunberg, the schoolgirl that, since August of 2018, has been on strike from school every Friday to demonstrate to the world that the climate crisis is more important than academic education. She advocates that in fact, academic education will be worthless on a planet that becomes inhabitable. Greta has inspired millions of others around the world, and her movement has pushed several governments to declare a climate emergency and begin acting to reverse climate change damage.

Additionally, a range of voices have come together from all paths of life to strengthen research initiatives, with the aim of discovering more encompassing solutions to address climate change and encourage innovation.

Governments and individuals must come together on this. We can't just delegate responsibility to global powers on these issues. Action needs to come from below as well as from above; we need collective action to fundamentally

---

7 You can read a very thoughtful blog post by MAD Challenges on this: madchallenges.org/a-response-to-climate-doom-and-gloom/

change the way we consume and use resources, until living within our means becomes the norm.

We have changed the course of history before; we can do it again. Individuals have greater power than we give them credit for, including ourselves.

Think about it: true leaders are people who manage, largely by themselves, to change the lives of thousands just by using their charisma, their sense of purpose, their drive, their perseverance, and the power of their minds.

Martin Luther King, Gandhi, Mother Theresa, and, dare I say, Greta Thunberg – the unexpected and unconventional hero of our times – have all but single-handedly moved thousands, if not millions, of people to action. Sometimes they have even changed the course of history with their strong beliefs and vision.

It is possible for you to do the same. You don't need a privileged background, top qualifications, or special powers. All these inspirational figures started with a passion, which was so all-consuming that they motivated thousands of others to join them.

All the same, you can act within your own circle of family, friends, and colleagues; join your local environmental charity; teach sustainability in local schools; or go tree-planting on the weekend. You can install renewable energy and heat sources in your home or switch to a 100% renewable energy provider. You can choose to use your bike instead of your car.

You don't have to become a hero, but you can certainly make a difference as an individual. After all, oceans are made of individual drops of water. With your values and behaviour, you can make an impression on others that may have unexpected and wonderful ripple effects for years to come.

The Power of an Idea

David Symons is the U.K. Director of Sustainability at WSP, one of the largest engineering consultancies in the world. David has been working in sustainability for nearly three decades.

A few years ago, David envisioned a programme that could benefit the many projects WSP had around the world. WSP is composed of over 48,000 employees at the time of writing. This programme would take into account future climate, future society, future resources, and future technology that could pose a challenge to those buildings - and, thus, Future Ready was born.

Not an easy task, but a necessary one.

Think about hospitals, like Trafford General Hospital. It was the first hospital that opened in the U.K. National Health Service in 1948, and upon its inception, it treated tuberculosis and World War II injuries only. These conditions are non-existent now, which - in theory - makes the hospital unfit for duty. Modern hospitals, however, not only treat present issues - but are designed to treat diseases of the future. The lifespan of buildings is predicted to stretch to 70 years and beyond, so they must be now prepared for heart disease; cancer; lifestyle illnesses like obesity and diabetes; geriatric care, including dementia; and many more.

Hospitals are not static places waiting to be left behind; they evolve to predict new conditions, prevent diseases, and prepare treatment for ailments yet to come. In an architectural context, this can also mean removing limitations in their design. For example: larger doors, less complex floor plans, better wayfinding, more colours to identify the spaces visually, fewer steps, more access to the outdoors, and more rehabilitation areas.

Modern designers also deal with very different climatic conditions, which affects the architectural evolution. Altogether, it becomes easy to see the plethora of challenges that future designers will have to deal with.

Why not prepare for the future, rather than undoing the past?

With that said, how do you convince such a large organisation that there are benefits to being "future ready"?

Since David had to sell at different levels and to various stakeholders, in a large organisation like WSP, he was forced to relentlessly push his idea on the company via huge communication exercises. When I interviewed him for Green Gorilla Conversations, he admitted that, at present, most of his time is spent engaging and presenting the same six slides to hundreds of people every year - especially new staff - because his programme is now a global reality. However, Future Ready is one of the key themes of WSP globally, not by chance, but through David continuously refining his idea and explaining the benefits at different levels.

David's story proves that, with the right amount of hard work and grit, you can achieve anything you believe in, even as an individual. It's not a matter of talent (although that helps), but rather of daily commitment to manifesting your ideas, no matter how long it takes to fulfil them. It isn't about overnight success, but the small action steps you take in order to achieve your goals.

Reframe the setbacks as growth points, instead of throwing in the towel at the first hurdle. You need to cultivate this growth mindset, so you can stick to your long-term goals without being completely levelled by your failures.

Key Points to Remember

Feel free to use this space for jotting down notes on your personal takeaways from this section.

CHAPTER 3

Making Peace with Being a Troublemaker

When I interviewed Jerry Yudelson for my Green Gorilla Conversations podcast[8], he was smiling wryly like the Cheshire Cat, thinking about how things had gone for him.

Jerry, dubbed 'the Godfather of Green' by *Wired* magazine in 2011, is a troublemaker.

With a long career as a pioneer of sustainability in the built environment, he was a forerunning LEED[9] Fellow, and one of the first to advise on and teach LEED in America. Yet, he's still a highly vocal critic of it. In spite of the ample praise LEED receives from all parts of the construction industry around the

---

8 www.thegreengorilla.co.uk/resources/videos

9 Leadership in Energy and Environmental Design, the leading environmental assessment tool for buildings in the U.S.

world, Jerry went under the skin of this very popular environmental assessment method. There he uncovered its faults and now confidently implements forensic analyses of how it failed.

The goal of LEED is to transform the marketplace.

However, looking at the statistics, he realised that many factors hindered its spread as a mass tool to assess environmental performance in buildings. These included, among other things: high costs, lengthy certification process, sometimes arbitrary rulings by review panels of "experts", detachment from the reality of building sites, and, almost exclusively, a focus on new buildings instead of operational ones.

This meant that, as of 2016, LEED certified only one billion square feet of offices in the United States. That sounds outstanding - until you realise it only represents 1% of the total U.S. office area, therefore hardly scratching the surface. The construction industry needs a drastic transformation in order to clean up its act and reduce carbon emissions - and 1% is not nearly sufficient.

Jerry has written insightful books on the sustainability industry in America, and he's a witty storyteller. He's not a corporate guy, and that pleases him immensely. For me, Jerry encompasses the true sustainability professional: a person who cares far too much for the environment and doing the 'right thing' to obey institutional rules. Because Jerry knows the industry inside-out, he can speak from a place of authority, not of arrogance.

As deeply passionate people with high values, I think it's important that we aren't ashamed of being troublemakers and wanting desperately to change the status quo. If anything, we need to value the fact that we often don't fit in.

A famous quote that has been attributed to Einstein goes: "Insanity is repeating the same mistakes and expecting different results". Although it might not be the great scientist's quote, this saying still holds a profound truth.

Humans are an extremely adaptable species, and that's helped us to both thrive in harsh conditions and reach this point in history. In modern times, we are adapting to high levels of pollution, both in our air and in our food; adapting to favour work or entertainment over sleep; adapting to become completely detached from nature by spending over 90% of our time indoors; adapting day by day to alarming climate changes. The trouble is: as a species, we often don't realise there's a problem (since changes can be slow and difficult to pin-point) or we don't think we're responsible for any of it. Worse yet, we often view course-correction as too much hassle, requiring levels of strength that the average human being doesn't possess.

Troublemakers are important; they see the world using an unconventional lens. Troublemakers question everything and do not adapt to patterns they view as harmful in the long run, even if they're a norm that people have learnt to swallow as a matter of fact. Troublemakers can be a pain to others who don't share the same values, instead wanting peace and quiet, but, in reality, in order to obtain peace and quiet again, disruption is necessary. It improves and changes direction when the status quo doesn't work.

So, how can we be *productive* troublemakers? People that actually contribute to the advancement of society, instead of just making noise?

Step one is to have a goal in mind - one in line with your values. Create this by identifying something that doesn't seem right in your world; in the case of Jerry Yudelson, it was the environmental assessment methods available for buildings, and the fact that they made an insufficient impact in decarbonising the construction industry. Then, try to focus on the solution, not the problem.

Is there an existing solution to your issue? If not, what is necessary to create one? Jerry compiled all the elements that would make the environmental assessments far more effective and widespread. With it, anyone who took the blueprint in their hands could create a new system to drive sustainability in buildings - with real results.[10]

If you can't alter (or revolutionise) the current system directly, who can? Do you need to write a book? Or speak to your boss, or your boss' boss? Or to the local authority? Or to the Prime Minister?

No matter how ambitious your goal, if the solution you've outlined is feasible at some level, you can find other people to believe and support it.

---

10   If you're interested, you can find it in *Reinventing Green Building*, Jerry's hugely inspirational book. J. Yudelson, *Reinventing Green Building: Why Certification Systems Aren't Working and What We Can Do About It*, New Society Publishers, 2016.

You can post videos or write about it, via blogs, articles in industry magazines, social media posts, or by directly engaging with people you think are relevant. But the most important thing is to be consistent.

Have you ever noticed how some Mr. Nobody gets millions of YouTube or Instagram followers, just because they consistently publish content? They've found their niche, and their followers eventually got the message by absorbing it on a regular basis. There's a well-known marketing rule of thumb that says we need to view a message seven times before we actually do something about it. So, you need to be consistently out there with your message before your audience takes notice and provides results.

Take again the example of Greta Thunberg. Greta started her first strikes by herself, in the company of her iconic '*Skolstrejk för klimatet*' hand-painted sign, outside the Swedish parliament. Consistently, every Friday, she would skip school until some people got curious and started following her. Her followers became millions and she ended up, only a few months later, speaking to the European Parliament, the Pope, Arnold Schwarzenegger, and Barack Obama (to name a few). Eventually, she prompted governments around the world to declare a climate emergency and start acting upon it as if "your house is on fire".

To better understand this fascinating phenomenon of leaders and followers, I invite you to watch the *First Follower: Leadership Lessons from Dancing Guy* on YouTube[11]. This video shows in a light-hearted way how you can be a leader (and influence others to join) if you have the guts to stand alone for a while, being ridiculed and considered a lone nut. If you keep at it, ensure your message is simple enough for others to absorb, and praise and nurture your first, all-important followers, sure enough: you will start a movement.

Another troublemaker I had the good fortune to interview was the admirable Martin Brown. Martin defines himself as an innovative sustainability 'provocateur'. In his career of over 40 years, he has authored the book *FutuREstorative, Working Towards a New Sustainability*[12], advised and worked on countless projects,

---

11 youtu.be/fW8amMCVAJQ

12 www.fairsnape.com/martin-brown-publications/

and co-founded the Living Future Institute Europe, which brings to Europe the Living Building Challenge[13] principles.

The Living Building Challenge is an environmental scorecard, first created in the U.S. in 2006. It motivates people to think in terms of absolute environmental benefits, not incremental or percentage improvements over existing norms. Based on two core principles, all "imperatives" are mandatory, and certification is based on actual performance, rather than modelled on anticipated performance. So, you either go all in (with zero net energy, zero mains water, zero combustion, avoiding ALL materials that can harm people or the environment, and so on) or you don't get certification for your building.

In fact, Martin is a pioneer of the Living Building Challenge, having advised on the first building in Europe to seek full-petal 'Living Certification': the Cuerden Valley Visitor Centre in Preston, Lancashire, U.K.

It takes an awful lot of commitment and creativity to make buildings that fulfil all the requirements, including, for example, only utilising materials that are not listed in the Living Building Challenge's Red List. When I interviewed him, Martin described how, instead of MDF, the project included panels made of timber and a glue composed of starch from potato peels.

Martin is one of these committed individuals who can see the end goal clearly and won't hesitate in the face of a disbelieving local authority or main contractor. He understands how repeating past mistakes will not support our environmental global objectives, which need radical actions and a completely renewed attitude.

---

13   www.living-future.org/lbc/

Key Points to Remember

Feel free to use this space for jotting down notes on your personal takeaways from this section.

CHAPTER 4

Why Aren't My Clients Interested in Sustainability?

The summer of 2018 was, at that point, declared "the hottest summer ever". Despite the scorching heat plaguing the planet and the ice caps melting at a never-before-seen rate, there were still naysayers of climate change.

Well-intended comments ranged from "Now and then, it happens" to "It's lovely, isn't it?"

Or is it? I was feeling slightly ungrateful. Yes, I was born in Sicily; a self-confessed lizard who used to spend hours frying in the sun whilst covered in baby oil (kids, do not try this at home) to get my skin just the right shade of brown. Heaven, please, save me from the consequences!

But *that* summer, in 2018, I didn't enjoy it.

There was something sinister in the brown leaves on the pavement, in the dry yellow grass, in the ant invasion afflicting my kitchen.

Perhaps because I felt like I *knew* what was happening. Perhaps because many moons ago, some apocalyptic scenarios were painted out for me by my university professors, which, at that time, felt a bit like 2001: *A Space Odyssey*. Is it really going to happen? Scorching heat, floods, hailstones as big as grapes, colder-than-normal temperatures in previously mild climates?

As you know by now, I chose a career in sustainability because I believed in it, not because it was fashionable. I believed in treating the planet kindly; in cleaner air and water; in peace and love. I am a tree hugger. These are my core values.

And, like me, other sustainability professionals feel the same drive to transform their values into a day job. What's better than working for eight hours a day (sometimes more) on what you're truly passionate about?

But reality hit me (and countless others) like a train to the face: not everyone shares the same values. Not everyone thinks that sustainability is obvious or wise. The person who inspired me to take up this career (and who also used to set his sink and WC on fire to clean them) once said to me:

"I don't want to call it 'sustainable design'. It is just architecture, done in the best, most common-sense way."

Right. If only.

Even today, whilst we sweat trying to finish a job with a fan pointed at our face (in the U.K.!), there are some clients who believe it will cost them astronomically more to implement sustainability, as compared to the standard capital costs they're used to. They don't understand the importance of implementing resilience strategies, so their buildings can survive the heaven-knows-what consequences of climate change.

If they do it, it's simply because the council imposed it on them. Are they really going to distribute that building user guide, which tells future tenants how to operate their building in an energy-efficient way? Are they really going to make sure everything works perfectly, so it has the smallest environmental impact in the long run?

Unfortunately, sustainability professionals are fighting against a harsh reality. Some will spend their days ticking little "yes" and "no" boxes in an environmental assessment, just for the sake of a certificate that will soon be forgotten. Feels like there's a large gap between values and common sense, and business. Or is there?

I've been asking myself this question over and over again: why aren't clients interested in sustainability?

Once, my then-eight-year-old daughter told me off, because we were still using plastic toothbrushes. I'm a sustainability consultant, and sustainability has been my daily life for over a decade now. Yet, I hadn't thought about the impact of disposable toothbrushes. She learnt at school that they were bad for the environment and would end up choking fish in the ocean.

I got the gist. It's undoubtedly true that plastic is too abundant in our oceans, so I immediately went and bought £3.50-a-pop bamboo toothbrushes. Eye-wateringly expensive compared to Wilko's four-for-£1, and the true impact of bamboo toothbrushes compared to plastic ones has not yet been fully investigated, but it seemed a less impactful decision, so I went with it.

I wonder if investors have inquisitive children asking them: daddy, mummy, what is the building you are building made of?

Or is money so powerful that it turns off even their most deeply rooted beliefs and values?

Having looked closely at the business case for sustainability when developing the Green Gorilla Masterclass Programme, in recent years, I've seen a definite shift in the perception of investing in sustainability. Investors are now able to track the high performers on ESG (Environmental, Social and Governance factors[14]) and are correlating better financial performance with better ESG performance. As a consequence, they're valuing those high performers more starkly.

---

14 These are sustainability factors like climate change and resource scarcity but also social issues like a company's labour practices, talent management, product safety and data security. ESG covers governance matters like board diversity, executive pay and business ethics. Investors increasingly rely on ESGs metrics to decide the risk levels of an investment.

Arabesque and the University of Oxford reviewed the academic literature on sustainability and corporate performance, and found that 90% (of the 200 studies analysed) conclude that good ESG standards will lower the cost of capital. Furthermore, 88% show that good ESG practices result in better operational performance, and 80% show that stock price performance is positively correlated with good sustainability practices.

Mark Carney, Governor of the Bank of England between 2013 and 2020, in his annual 2019 speech, said that the finance of the future will need to facilitate the transition into a carbon-neutral economy. He emphasised that this isn't just fundamental - it's existential. He also predicted that carbon-reporting for corporations via the TCFD[15] will need to become mandatory for this to happen.

However, at the level where we, the sustainability practitioners, generally work, the majority of clients are still refusing to embrace the change.

It can be tough, standing in front of people that have already dismissed what you believe in; or who don't want to collaborate; or who think that, because they pay you, you should do it for them.

But it's important to actively listen to your clients' concerns and understand why they have an initial negative response to sustainability. If you understand their perspective, you can better respond to it. You could even manage to swing their perception from negative to positive.

I conclude that there are at least four reasons why our clients don't "get" sustainability, and not all of them are to do with money:

1. Apathy Mixed with Busy-ness

Clients are not in-tune with occurrences at a global level. The penny hasn't dropped yet with regards to connecting their business activities to the climate crisis. They have enough on their plate, just keeping their heads above water; they can't also bother with ethical concerns.

---

15   Task Force on Climate-related Financial Disclosures

2. Unawareness

So far, perhaps no-one has managed to explain to them the business case for sustainability in a way they can fully understand. They don't know that sustainability can help save money, big time.

Sustainability professionals – especially consultants - often jump into explaining the finer details: How they should engage with a qualified ecologist ASAP; how wide the cycle lanes should be; how many products are covered by EPD (Environmental Product Declaration) certificates, and so on. They fail to outline the bigger picture.

Sustainability consultants may often be preoccupied with achieving the final BREEAM or LEED rating and certificate, but fail to see the bigger picture themselves. Perhaps they lost sight of it. Perhaps the bigger picture initially drove them to this career, but they lost that simple message under a mountain of details. If that's the truth, how can they inspire their clients?

3. Fear of Change

It's a very basic human instinct to preserve the status quo. Neuroscientist Dr. David Rock created a model to help people assess their initial reaction to change, so they could pinpoint exactly why they felt threatened by it.

When your clients refuse to embrace sustainability, they likely have one or more of these five concerns:

- Is the change going to alter my perceived status?

- I'm not sure how the future will look if we adopt the change.

- What if I lose control over what I'm doing?

- Who will I be working with, and what will that change?

- Is it fair?

Could your client have these concerns?

4. Biased Opinion

Clients may have a flawed perception about the real costs of implementing sustainability, and think it requires great effort for very little gain. They might be asking themselves and you: what are the advantages? What is the return on investment?

There is a clear method for dealing with your clients and this specific issue, as well as tailoring your responses to them. I will discuss that in Part 2 of this book. For now, let me explain this client concern in more depth:

When debating this argument on LinkedIn[16], another consultant correctly pointed out that ours is a death-phobic culture. We are permitted (encouraged, even) to behave as if each of us will live forever.

This allows us all to live a two-fold life. We discuss sustainability with genuine, deep concern, and then return to our usual lives as if nothing bad has happened or ever will. Given a choice between existential crisis and denial, only a small handful will ever choose the former. It takes deeply ingrained personal values to truly act on something that we might never see the results of.

Your clients may have one or more of these four concerns. How they manifest and act on these fears, however, is less simple. Your clients are not all created equal.

Clients, and stakeholders in general (i.e. people you need to work with as part of the project), come in three kinds.

Let me illustrate this with an example borrowed from the construction industry and my personal experience, but I'm sure you can picture the same type of clients in your own industry.

The Sustainability Advocate

These are clients who work for businesses that have sustainability at their heart - the Co-op, Body Shop and WholeFoods of this world. They make a point of having sustainable buildings that are the physical demonstration of their companies' values. CSR is a fundamental part of their business operations, and they have strong environmental policies.

---

16   You are most welcome to connect with me on LinkedIn: www.linkedin.com/in/
virginiacinquemani/

You will have an easy ride with these clients. They want the most sustainable buildings possible, the most environmentally-conscious business operations, and they will work with you to make it happen. They've allocated a reasonable budget, have done their research, and may even know more than you in certain cases.

They may want to achieve the highest-ever score in a sustainability assessment, or go for several types of assessments (LEED, BREEAM, WELL, Living Building Challenge…) to create a real landmark. Exciting times!

The Law-Abiding

This type of client knows that they *have* to go through a sustainability traffic light, perhaps by carrying out a sustainability assessment on their building. They know it's a condition for planning permission and, therefore, don't necessarily approve of it, but will do it anyway.

You may have to explain what the sustainability assessment entails, because they're unaware. With that said, they're usually happy to support you to reach the sustainability objectives of their projects.

If things get tough, however (e.g. unexpected budget constraints), they may not want to proceed with certain features that you advised. The sustainability assessment might be scaled down to a mere tick-box exercise to comply with the council's rules.

The Naysayer

Your worst nightmare. This client only wants to make money, and quickly. The building is a short-term investment for them, and they don't care about integrating sustainability with the project; they just want to create the building and make a profit.

You will have a hard time convincing them to perform at least an environmental assessment on the building, let alone develop a wider sustainability strategy. They won't see its value and don't want to spend money on it. Perhaps they appointed you at the very last minute, because they realised they *need* to perform an assessment, but they aren't ready to invest so as to reap the benefits. They want you to bend the rules; to create evidence out of thin air.

I am rooting for you, believe me.

On a personal level, most seem generally affected by bad news surrounding climate change. However, on a business level, they may think it's not worth the effort and that, unfortunately, there are more pressing issues to deal with.

As mentioned before, they could also fail to understand what sustainability really is - and they aren't the only ones.

Once, not long ago, I was invited to deliver a Continuous Professional Development session on Sustainable Design at a small architectural studio.

Beforehand, I was told that the office didn't specifically embed sustainability in their *modus operandi,* as it was a small practice.

In my head, that sounded very much like the excuse I'd heard countless times when, at the beginning of my career, I worked at a small architectural practice myself. What does being a small practice have to do with the opportunity to design sustainable buildings?

When I was working in architecture, it was a different time, and sustainability was still a fancy, cryptic practice that only a few visionary architects explored. Today, I'm wondering whether designers can actually afford not to consider sustainability in their work. What do they actually think it means to build sustainably?

I wanted to find out. So, that was my first question when I arrived at the CPD session:

"Have you ever considered sustainability in your practice?"

The answer was:

"Uhm, yeah, well, a few years ago, we considered putting photovoltaic panels on one building, but you know, the costs were high, so in the end, we didn't."

I then realised that it's not just ordinary people, but also built-environment professionals who view sustainability as a fancy add-on. Nothing has really changed since the early Noughties, when I still worked in an architectural practice.

Businesses claimed they were operating in 'green' ways, when they weren't.

I still remember a promotional campaign in 2007, where the Honda Racing Formula 1 Team launched their RA107 F1 car. In place of the advertising and sponsor logos, it featured a huge image of the Earth "to help raise awareness of the environmental issues facing the planet". *Seriously?*

Add to this those leading governments (like the U.S.) who shy away from international treaties, like the Paris Agreement, on the basis that it would undermine their national economy. This sends the message that money is more important, or, worse still, that the economy and the environment are separate businesses.

Over two decades of green washing haven't helped either. Even sector specialists now avoid using the word "sustainability" like the plague (it went down the pan along with "green" and "eco"), and rather use "future" and "innovation". For an example in recent years, a major U.K. sector exhibition, EcoBuild, has now been rebranded FutureBuild.

However, not all hope is lost. Because you work in the sector, you probably know that Scotland has become a world leader in sourcing its electricity from renewables. In 2017, the nation received more than two-thirds (68.1%) of its electricity from green schemes – an increase of 26% on the year before.

Additionally, as Ocean Unite has pointed out, the ocean is probably the largest business on the planet. It's the world's seventh largest economy with a "GDP" equivalent to $2.5 trillion USD (about 5% of the global GDP). It's estimated that strongly protecting 30% of the ocean would cost about $225 billion USD, but the financial net benefits could be as much as $920 billion USD by 2050. Protecting the ocean makes financial - as well as environmental and moral - sense.

However, talk of the successful marriage between economy and sustainability has yet to become mainstream.

On one hand, many breakthrough practices *have* become mainstream, with the advancement of national building regulations, climate acts, and rising awareness amongst the general public, with plastic-free movements, products, and initiatives multiplying every day around the globe.

On the other hand, CO_2 emissions rise instead of going down in many countries - with the U.S. and China topping the chart. Our climate is transforming at an alarming rate. Yet, naysayers are still in positions of power, and it's very hard to make sustainability a priority when action doesn't come from above.

Now, it is your job, as a sustainability professional, to set the record straight and open your clients' eyes to a new way of thinking.

In order to do that, you need to understand your clients' concerns, and that means really listening to them (I will discuss how to enhance your listening skills later on in this book). It's also your job to transform their concerns into opportunities. You must respond to their needs with your well-honed pitch that sustainability is the key to putting their fears to rest.

The magic fix? Showing clients and other naysayers in the boardroom that there is money to be found in sustainability - and, what's more, that it makes good sense for them, their reputation, and their future business to implement sustainability in their projects.

But you need to believe in it. You need to show yourself and the world what you believe in, and become a leader in this new way of thinking.

Key Points to Remember

Feel free to use this space for jotting down notes on your personal takeaways from this section.

CHAPTER 5

When Winds Change, Opportunity Knocks

In his 2019 speech, Mark Carney declared that "the changes required to achieve the zero-carbon targets that the U.K. Government have set for 2050 are enormous. Carbon emissions will have to decline by 45% from 2010 levels over the next decade. This will require a massive reallocation of capital and creating unprecedented risks and opportunities. As one example, it is estimated that annual investment in sustainable infrastructure could top £20 billion for decades. Firms that align their business models to the transition to a carbon-neutral world will be rewarded handsomely; those that fail to adapt will cease to exist."

And, with your technical expertise, you can be a part of that change.

Unless you've lived under a rock in the past few years, you're aware that the news focuses on ice melting, freak weather accidents, observations on the 'hottest summer ever', and many other alarming events.

It's a grim outlook. However, there's good news: by focusing the public's attention on the issue and pressuring decision-makers at a global level, real action is being kickstarted. From a business point of view, you might still struggle with clients and individuals who are difficult to convince, but evidence suggests that big corporations have already understood the new opportunity being presented.

You can be part of that opportunity.

Environmental concerns about social issues, the climate crisis, rising inequality, and poor working conditions all demand action from political leaders, businesses, and individuals at a global level.

One key sign of change is the creation of the Task Force on Climate-related Financial Disclosures (TCFD). Established in 2015 by the Financial Stability Board (FSB), it's tasked with developing voluntary, consistent, climate-related financial risk disclosures for use by companies, banks, and investors in providing information to stakeholders. In the words of Michael Bloomberg, American politician, founder of Bloomberg LP, and chair of the TCFD and UN special envoy for climate action: "The more companies know about the risks they face, the faster and more effectively they can address them – and the more they report that information, the better equipped investors will be to make smart decisions."

Investor-pressure and the TCFD are clear evidence that sustainability is becoming critical to long-term business and value creation.

Green finance has grown exponentially in recent years, and whilst it still only accounts for less than 10% of global finance (at the time of writing), investors - driven by greater awareness from the sector, as well as public calls for firms to divest away from fossil fuels - now know that climate change is not a theoretical concern. This has a strong impact on the resilience of investor portfolios.

Moreover, it's likely that corporations around the world will be increasingly forced to disclose climate data as a legislative requirement.

But it's not only large corporations that have begun shifting perspective.

The press also has strong interpretations regarding companies' quiet switch from conventional to more sustainable methods of producing their goods. For example, that it indicates "sustainability is not cool" for consumers that can't stand the term or the hippy associations with it. Their actions could be interpreted as greenwash.

Winemakers, clothing labels, organic grocery producers; many are changing their practices to ditch pesticides and artificial fertilisers, and they are not shouting about it. My personal view is that sustainability is finally becoming an indicator of quality and responsibility (what business wants to be seen as irresponsible?). This gives businesses an advantage in the fiercely competitive marketplace we live in. They want to continue business as usual, and ensure longevity to their activities and high standards for their customers.

Years ago, I met a wine producer in Sicily that used only organic manure and natural pesticides in his vinery, yet didn't have the 'organic' label on his wines. Why? Because going through the controls and processes of the Organic Soil Association (or any other organic labelling association) can be too expensive, lengthy, and cumbersome for small growers. Likewise, these small businesses might not be marketing savvy.

Just because companies aren't shouting about their clean conscience, doesn't mean they're not doing the right thing.

Since 2009, Innocent Drinks has been researching how to support their supply chain of fruit growers to overcome the challenges of climate change. For years, they've experienced unreliable and often disastrous weather patterns.

In the areas where Alphonso mangoes are grown in India, for example, Innocent developed a simple five-step organic programme, in partnership with local Indian universities:

1. Use of organic manure.

2. Reduction of the canopy effect from higher branches and trees.

3. Natural pest control.

4. Monitoring of fruit development.

5. Irrigation.

This programme has resulted in bigger yields, healthier trees, and both larger and better-quality fruits. The side effect is that, of course, farmers make more money and enjoy a better quality of life.

Yet the argument we hear often is that implementing sustainability is expensive - even more so at a large scale (i.e. by revolutionising our economic system entirely).

The chair of the IPCC, Dr. Hoesung Lee, has calculated that going net-zero carbon would only require a 0.4% supplementary investment on the current global GDP spent on energy. This seems trivial compared to the catastrophic fallout of inaction, as highlighted over a decade ago by the Stern Report. Within it, among other issues, were heavier floods and droughts; hundreds of millions of people being flooded and permanently displaced due to rising sea levels; and 15 to 40% of species facing extinction.

From a purely economic point of view, climate change means serious damage to property and critical infrastructure, as well as negative impacts on human health, productivity, and on sectors such as agriculture, forestry, fisheries, and tourism. A recent study from the U.S. Environmental Protection Agency projected that, if the higher-temperature scenario prevails, its impact on a wide variety of sectors could cost the U.S. alone $520 billion each year.

Dr. Lee advocates that is a lack of political will, not of economic availability, that is stopping global action from taking place. It's quite obvious that many countries and key individuals still have a huge invested interest in fossil fuels, which makes it hard to divert focus to cleaner energy sources.

But, again, traditionally risk-averse sectors - like financial services - are turning a corner with the birth of the Green Finance Institute in the U.K., as well as similar bodies around the world. They encourage and mobilise new green finance projects spanning an array of sectors. Additionally, national banks and finance giants (encouraged by the data surrounding risks in the insurance sector) are now increasingly on board. They see the opportunity in offering green investment and lending products, from mortgages to pensions to loans.

We're also seeing a huge divestment from fossil - into the trillions. Not only does climate change policy make it high-risk, but the price of renewables is falling when combined with oil and gas price volatility.

Climate change is worth trillions in growth and new jobs creation.

Think about smart cities, clean energy, circular economy, sustainable land use, and water and waste management. Each of these elements constitutes a huge, profitable opportunity for thousands of people. The world needs expertise to deliver these new paradigms, and it is only a matter of time before the focus is almost entirely on these issues.

You can be a part of this huge opportunity.

But if you want to have an edge, and make it in an increasingly competitive world, you need to be prepared. You need to develop a combination of technical expertise and soft skills to sell the right solutions, as well as strengthen your resilience in a rapidly changing world.

Key Points to Remember

Feel free to use this space for jotting down notes on your personal takeaways from this section.

CHAPTER 6

Find Meaning in Your Day Job

Hopefully, you can now see that there's another method of approaching the challenges of being a sustainability professional. You can make a difference.

I recently encountered the concept of *Ikigai* - or, *reason for being* - which originated in the Japanese island of Okinawa, said to be home to the largest population of centenarians in the world. Ikigai appears to be a prime reason why Okinawans live happy, longer-than-average lives.

This concept can be translated to our work scenario as finding your *"sweet spot"* in life. Here, "what you love" *and* "what you're good at" meets "what the world needs" and "what you can get paid for".

If sustainability is the convergence of these four elements for you, then it looks like you've found your Ikigai.

When I interviewed Martin Gettings, Head of Sustainability at Canary Wharf Group, for the Green Gorilla Conversations series, he mentioned Ikigai to me as a method to check if what he does is still fulfilling. You should do that if you feel your job has lost its glow.

Agreed, it may not always be possible. Sometimes you just have to pay the bills and you might not love what you do. However, ideally, that's what you strive for: long-term professional (and personal) satisfaction.

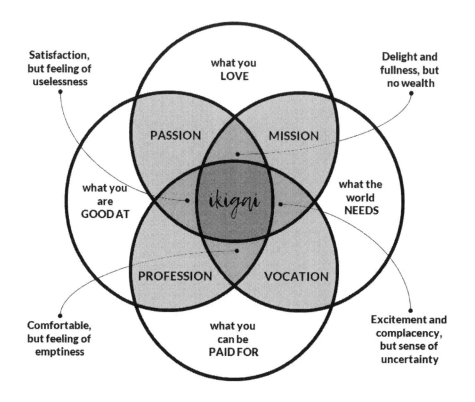

Ikigai, a Japanese concept meaning "a reason for being"

I invite you to look at the image above and mark where you think you are right now.

Perhaps you love what you do, and the contribution you make to the world, but you're at a low pay rate? (That's, by the way, the majority of sustainability professionals.)

Or maybe you haven't found your place in the world yet, and have a feeling of emptiness?

In both cases, the best step forward is by setting meaningful goals to achieve your vision. Start by taking a look at where you are and where you want to be. Then, aim to find a happy compromise, where:

+ You are satisfied with how your skills are used to benefit the world.

+ You do something that you love.

+ You are being paid for it.

If you've found your Ikigai, I invite you to cherish that. Then, use it to tap into your passion and beliefs when you speak to your next client (without sounding like a preacher at the speakers' corner of Hyde Park, of course). But when you believe in it, others will too.

"People don't buy what you do; they buy why you do it," author Simon Sinek tells us in his TED talk and book, "Start with the Why"[17]. It's also part of the fine art of storytelling, which is an ultimate skill for a successful sustainability consultant (as we'll see later in this book). The bottom line is: not all professions are created equal, and we are lucky to be involved in something that can make a real difference to the world around us.

The impact our profession can have is massive and long-lasting - even just one project at a time. That's worth reflecting on, especially if you feel uninspired right now.

Green Gorilla Conversations

For more inspiring stories of sustainability professionals who made it that extra mile, take a look at Green Gorilla's website and the "Resources' section, where you'll find a selection of Green Gorilla Conversations. I've interviewed many masters of sustainability, asking them about their recipe for success, including Martin Gettings, David Symons, Jerry Yudelson, Kartik Amrania, and more.[18]

Key Points to Remember

Feel free to use this space for jotting down notes on your personal takeaways from this section.

CHAPTER 7

How to Keep Your Passion Alive

If sustainability was something that you chose when you were 17 - when you still had a head full of auburn hair - you might find yourself, after a few years, not 'feeling' it in the same way.

I have to admit, at one point, that was me.

For some people, when kids come along, that means becoming a green ninja. They try to protect their children's future by reducing their own impact on the environment.

For me, life became busier, and the training job I held at the time - with the office politics and the day-to-day pressures to make a profit - wasn't inspiring me like my previous job. I lost interest. Even though I was trying to be a good citizen in my private life, I didn't make sustainability my priority.

As a consequence, for a few years, my profession was just a job to pay the bills.

Often, money and ideals don't combine well. For a start, I am an idealist. What gets me up in the morning is the need to make a difference in the world, and to make my family and myself proud - not strictly speaking, to make money.

Most sustainability professionals want to primarily make a difference, not money. Otherwise, we would be talking stock and shares and working in finance right now.

However, like you, I'm still learning that money is a necessary part of the equation and shouldn't be frowned upon.

You could also be involved in sustainability work on a voluntary basis (Me? I'm part of my city's sustainability group, which includes bringing a sustainability programme for children into the local schools, which I aptly called Green Monkey). However, if you chose this as your profession, then you need to account for making money and providing for your lifestyle. Money and profit are likely why most of your clients are engaging with you; they want sustainability to have a return on their investment in some way or another.

But what if you need to maintain a profession that now lacks the appeal it had a few years ago, when you first chose it? What do you do?

In my conversations with the masters of sustainability, I always ask that question.

Because I know; it's not easy to connect with your ideals and your passion when clients aren't interested in what you're saying. You're battling to finish an assessment when you know it won't make a difference. The measures will not be implemented in reality; or bureaucracy is killing your ideas; or your boss wants you to make a profit; or you're a technical person and don't know when to start with business development.

Our colleagues that 'made it' in sustainability reckon you should strive and make a conscious effort to keep your passion alive – unless of course, you decide to give everything up and open a cocktail bar on a Mexican beach.

But, if that's not you, then read on.

Keep Learning

David Symons, Director of Sustainability in the U.K. for WSP, suggests reading industry magazines and media coverage to keep abreast of changes and stay in the middle of the debate.

Be curious, explore outside your industry, and find parallels that you can apply to sustainability.

Do Something Different From Your Day-to-Day Job

Dave Cheshire, Regional Director of Sustainability for AECOM, suggests engaging in something which fuels your passion in your spare time. He's written many articles, and that led him to write the excellent book *Building Revolutions: Applying the Circular Economy to the Built Environment.* If writing isn't your forte, you could plant trees, support the local WWF branch, or make art from recycled waste; anything that helps you reconnect with that passion, without the stress of making a profit.

Don't Rely on Motivation

An unpopular but vital point to consider is that motivation is very overrated. We hear about motivation every January, whilst trying to stick to our New Year's resolutions. But once motivation to boost your career, start new habits, read more, or eat healthier, fades – and it does - everything stops and you return to dear old comfort.

It's human nature.

In my experience, the best way to make lasting changes is to think about what *type of person you want to be.*[19]

If you want to transform the kind of sustainability professional you are, then start being intentional about your life, inside and outside of work.

---

19 If you are interested in learning more, I suggest you read *Atomic Habits,* by James Clear, a wonderful and practical book to help you make habits stick. J. Clear, *Atomic Habits:Tiny Changes, Remarkable Results.* Penguin Random House Business, 2018

I heard someone say that 100% commitment is easier than 98%. And it is.

Since founding my company and taking full ownership of my career I, for example, became more conscious of my food choices. Years ago, I switched to a pescatarian diet because of the impact meat production has on the planet's resources – but also, to be perfectly honest, because I didn't like eating meat.

After a year into entrepreneurship, sustainability returned as such a powerful drive in my life - so much so, even that diet didn't feel in line with my values, so I became a vegan. At first, I committed to eating only plant-based foods. Then I realised it was a colossal shift in identity. In time, I managed to call myself a vegan, because I embraced that it was the kind of person I wanted to be.

I realised that I am one person; what goes on at work trickles into my personal life and vice versa. My values, not the prospect of a wealthy future, made me choose sustainability - and those values don't stop at my front door.

It's all down to personal choice, values, and intentionality. Own who you want to be.

Whether that's being a gym enthusiast or someone who unwinds with a glass of wine in front of a movie each evening, don't be incidental about it. If you dislike the persona you're enacting right now, change it.

Are you the type of person who waits for inspiration to visit the gym? Or the person who prepares their gym kit and places it in front of their door the night before, so it becomes automatic to grab it and go for a workout?

The goal here is to avoid daily decision fatigue. Establish intentionality in the person you want to be once and for all, and build your life around small incremental changes until you become that person. Even if you're not that person right now - but you'd love to be - you can fake it until you make it. I promise, it works.

The main trick is to show up consistently. It won't make a difference all the time, and you may just do five push-ups at first, but that's already better than zero push-ups. Showing up creates consistency, and eventually carries you to that aspirational level - one small habit at a time.

You can do the same with your career.

Are you the type of person who:

- Wants to make a difference to the environment?

- Reads one sector magazine a week to keep up with the industry?

- Gets engaged in local activities?

- Is in constant 'learning mode'?

- Gets involved with their membership organisation?

- Inspires their clients to do good *as well as* make a profit?

The choice is entirely yours.

Key Points to Remember

Feel free to use this space for jotting down notes on your personal takeaways from this section.

CHAPTER 8

What If I Can't Make an Impact?

Some of you may have chosen this book because you're at the start of your career. Or, you're still studying and want to prepare for the world of sustainability once you finish your formal education.

You might not have even spoken to a client yet. Or, if you have, you felt like a fraud; like you didn't have the right to be there.

Impostor Syndrome is a recognised phenomenon that affects people at all levels of their career. It was first identified in 1978 by psychologists Pauline Clance and Suzanne Imes.

According to some estimates, up to 70% of successful people have experienced Impostor Syndrome, including Maya Angelou, Albert Einstein, and Meryl Streep. Unlike other forms of anxiety that sap confidence, the syndrome's insidious nature makes you downplay your successes. You feel you are worthless or know less than anyone else in the room; those successes are just a trick you are playing on everybody else.

Perhaps you went to an event and felt uncomfortable when, as a young, enthusiastic environmental practitioner, you entered a stuffy room, full of people double your age with shiny shoes and smart ties, smiling broadly and patting each other on the back, calling themselves by first name. You have a feeling that you don't belong there; that you know less than everyone else; that you would rather be filling in spreadsheets and hiding behind your screen than doing *this*.

I know that feeling very well. Back in my architecture days, in addition to being a woman, a foreigner, young, and working in the construction industry (i.e. a sort of prize cow back then), I was a "relator" (according to the Clifton StrengthsFinder test[20]). This means I thrive when I'm with people I know well, and struggle uncomfortably with networking situations. In fact, although I'm quite extroverted, networking situations always made me so uneasy that I'd end up talking to my glass of wine and showing an unusual interest in the pictures on the wall (smartphones hadn't been invented yet).

Beyond this, Imposter Syndrome can also find you in the boardroom. In meetings, perhaps you can't seem to get your voice heard. Everyone else is louder, more confident, and appears to speak far more sense than you. If you do manage to say something, your ideas get dismissed or someone else begins talking instead.

It can depend on your perceived position in the room; you might be a junior among seniors, you might feel you're a minority (such as the only woman in the room), or you're simply introverted and despise these situations.

It's frustrating, but there is something you can do about it.

- ◆ **Step One:** Ask yourself what's holding you back.

Do you really need to develop new skills before you can speak, or are you just worried you're not good enough? Once you've identified the root to your lack of confidence, you can address it.

---

20   www.gallup.com/cliftonstrengths

♦ **Step Two:** Confirm Reality

It's helpful to recognise that your mind may be overplaying the situation. The movie running in your head is made of fictitious characters that judge and make you feel uncomfortable. While it may be true, it can also be an exaggeration. Take a moment to decide.

♦ **Step Three:** Cut Yourself a Break

Start by recognising that you're a work-in-progress – we all are – and that perfection doesn't exist. You may be new to the industry, or you may lack the confidence to speak up, but your opinion could bring a different perspective to the table. Perhaps it's a fresh solution that no-one else thought about before.

♦ **Step Four:** Be Willing to Learn From Mistakes

Even if your ideas are not original or end up not being the right fit for the issue at hand, practice and hone your trade. After all, you work in an industry that is intricate and constantly evolving - so embrace imperfection.

Sustainability is a complex subject, with new technology and new solutions coming up every day. It's impossible to know it all, so recognise your limits and see them as an opportunity to improve. Fuel your passion for learning, and love the process.

Step Five: Learn New Skills

With all that said, if you (like my 24-year-old self) are still not happy networking or speaking in front of many strangers (even just your boss and colleagues), it may be useful to learn some techniques to overcome these unpleasant feelings.

Whilst looking for leadership and management talents to help assemble the Green Gorilla Masterclass Programme (GGMP) and its training courses, I was intrigued by the personal story of Susan Heaton-Wright[21]. This incredible lady knows the type of confidence and skills required to speak in various situations with clarity and authenticity. Beyond that, she understands how to make an impact and compel people to listen. She draws knowledge from her former ca-

---

21   www.superstarcommunicator.com

reer as a professional international opera singer, singing in front of thousands of individuals and a full orchestra.

When Susan was at college, she was incredibly shy. When it was her turn at the school assembly, she would pay other pupils to stand up and lead it on her behalf. But she developed her resilience over the years; by hook or by crook, she had to learn to be comfortable performing in front of large audiences and the media.

She has now used that wealth of experience to create a communication programme, called the Superstar Communicator®, a method based on five specific areas: Audience, Preparation, Voice, Content, and Performance. She has taught the staff of corporations like CISCO, BRE, Marriott, Ernst and Young, and many more.

According to Susan, there is an effective, basic, and yet overlooked method (even by veteran professionals!) for relaxing in uncomfortable situations when you have to speak: preparing beforehand.

Do your homework.

If it's a meeting, prepare a simple bullet point list of things to say, so if your mind goes blank, you can quickly remind yourself of the key topics to discuss.

If it's a networking situation, then:

◆ Learn who will be present beforehand.

◆ Target a few interesting people you can learn from.

◆ Actively listen to what they say.

This will have a double advantage; you'll feel less like an outsider, because you'll be familiar with the attendee list, and you can prepare a few questions that are custom-tuned to your audience (try taking a cue about people's careers and interests on LinkedIn, without invading their privacy).

That's where you start.

From BREEAM Assessor to Green Gorilla

Andromaque had an experience similar to mine.

She's Greek but lives in France with her family, and she's a BREEAM assessor and sustainability consultant. She was one of the first to undertake the Green Gorilla Masterclass Programme.

You'd think it's only graduates fresh out of university and people with little experience that need to hone their soft skills, or who struggle with board meetings and hard-to-crack clients. However, a woman with over 10 years' practice in the sector can experience the same Impostor Syndrome as young graduates, despite the fact that she knows her stuff.

Andromaque is one of the oldest BREEAM assessors and knows the technical guide inside-out. However, she still struggled to convince her clients to fully embrace sustainability in their projects. From my personal experience, being a woman in the construction industry is still a bumpy road, at times, so that might have influenced the way Andromaque struggled.

So, she turned to Green Gorilla to address her issues. When I interviewed her after the programme, Andromaque shared that she picked this course to learn how to influence people without forcing them, and to better understand others.

In that sense, she found the Make an Impact module particularly useful. Through it, she realised that being assertive doesn't mean being arrogant. She loved the Become a Superstar Communicator module, where she learnt to pause and listen to her clients before launching into solution mode. At the end of the programme, she found a renewed sense of ownership of her ideas via the exercises designed to apply these concepts into her working life.

And this helped her step into her clients' shoes. Interestingly, she now manages to detach from her emotions; temporarily park the issues her clients might not want to hear about (namely, the ethical arguments, climate change, and other 'controversial' hot topics); and she attends meetings with the aim to both reach her goals and win the decision she needs.

As part of her homework, before meetings, she considers what she can wear to make herself feel more powerful in the boardroom - whether that's a favourite colour, or a business suit to match those of her male counterparts.

Key Points to Remember

Feel free to use this space for jotting down notes on your personal takeaways from this section.

PART2

The Top Five Skills

I studied architecture because I wanted to be an architect. Sounds obvious, right? Back in the day, you chose to study medicine because you wanted to be a doctor; engineering to become an engineer; law to become a lawyer.

My generation - Generation X as they call it, bordering on Millennial - is the first that often ended up with a different career than what they studied. Out of a circle of 10 friends who studied in my same School of Architecture, only three actually work as architects full-time. Others, including myself, have taken interesting related paths: one designs and produces furniture, one does interior design, one produces marketing videos, and I am a sustainability consultant and coach. Others have become school and university teachers.

My background is technical and I never thought I would need anything else, aside from learning about the Golden Ratio or Vitruvius' three principles of good architecture: *Firmitas* (Durability), *Utilitas* (Utility), and *Venustas* (Beauty).

Vitruvius, though, forgot to teach us how to speak to our clients. Or how to price and manage a job. In the first century B.C., did Vitruvius have obnoxious clients or the Mafia to deal with? Did he have to find a unique selling point in order to promote his architectural services? One thing's for sure: Vitruvius didn't grow up in a country overflowing with talented architects, and didn't have to emigrate to another country for a better prospect of life. Italy was a very different country then.

Having worked in the industry for a while, I realise I wasn't alone in thinking that technical skills were all I needed to succeed.

The majority of people who work in sustainability focus on training in technical subjects, and accumulate qualifications and badges to boost their CVs:

Masters and MBAs in sustainability, ESG and CSR reporting, waste management, social impact assessment, ISO 14001 auditing, BREEAM, LEED, WELL, Living Building Challenge, PassivHaus, and more. You may have encountered and even trained in some of them, which means you're qualified to carry out your job competently.

However, the variables and challenges we experience now, and the type of work we do, change very rapidly. If you're in the U.K. or the U.S., you have competition - and lots of it. Or, perhaps, you work in a country where sustainability is still news to people, so you may be working twice as hard to pioneer and explain to people why they should incorporate sustainability in their projects.

As such, you have to maintain your technical knowledge on a constant basis, above and beyond your formal training. However, you may have also come to realise (since you're reading this book) that knowing the energy yield of PV panels or the COP of heat pumps won't get you far in winning a job. In order to use that technical knowledge best, you need to develop other complementary skills which, arguably, have a *bigger* impact on the success of your career.

I first realised this when I was working at the BRE Academy. We used to deliver a plethora of technical courses, ranging from BREEAM, to fire doors, to BIM. Great content; generally happy clients.

However, day to day, when I supported members as Membership Manager and Head of Strategic Partnerships, I also saw our customers struggling. I could see them trapped between two huge fires: BREEAM (science-focussed, multi-layered, robust, and inflexible at times) and their clients (disinterested, pragmatic, focussed on profit). They struggled to bridge and intercede between the two, sometimes with little chance of success.

Communication breakdowns were common, with clients failing to understand how the system (and its various nuances) worked, and BREEAM being so cumbersome and complex that couldn't flex to accommodate specific needs. Would yet another course on energy or responsible sourcing of materials help those consultants? No.

Fast forward to today.

As mentioned earlier, as part of the Green Gorilla Conversations podcast, I've been interviewing people at the highest levels of their career, like company directors and MDs, about the evolutions of their jobs. Many of them have worked in sustainability for upwards of three decades. Their career journey typically evolved from technical (or even operative on building sites), to commercial, to PR. Now, they mostly accept invitations to talk publicly as the face of their organisation; they are keynote speakers at conferences, but they also talk to new starters and other employees about the company's values, ethos, and projects' aims. These days, they rarely get bogged down in details.

Communication is key in their profession. But is communication just opening your mouth and letting your vocal cords do the rest? Of course not.

Their communication entails not only explaining what their company does, what sustainability is, and so on, but also *selling* to people. Selling their company's values and services; selling sustainability; selling themselves – in the broadest sense of the term. They are motivational speakers. They are forced to slow down, then find and use their inner charisma. They have to reinvent themselves as spokespeople and gurus.

But communication is not only a skill necessary for those at the top of their careers. In fact, communication is key at every stage. Without effective communication, it's far more difficult to carry out any task without it ending up in disaster.

Here, I realised that the bulk of sustainability professionals - especially consultants in the U.K., but seemingly everywhere – haven't gone through proper soft skills training or screening.

In our profession, we focus heavily on only teaching the technical facts, leaving out important skills necessary for success. Our industry is plagued by acronyms and technicalities. In a world where the pace of technology is shrinking our attention span, capturing people's attention is far more difficult. In fact, a recent study suggests that, in meetings, workers are unable to focus on what's being said for longer than 13 minutes before zoning out.

IEMA, the leading alliance of environment and sustainability professionals, is one of the largest organisations to have noticed this gap early on. In 2011, they implemented a Sustainability Skills Map, which centres around: technical knowledge and sustainable governance principles; effective management; policy and regulatory knowledge; and, finally, personal skills, including effective communication, analytical thinking, and relationship development.

In a study conducted by McDonalds, the fast food chain, in 2015, it emerged that soft skills contribute £88 billion to the U.K. economy. In total, 97% of employers interviewed believed that soft skills were important to their current business success, whilst over half said that skills like communication and teamwork were more important than academic results. Even still, three-quarters of them believed there was a 'gap' of such skills in the U.K. workforce.

IEMA suggests that communication, decision making, self-management, teamwork, professionalism, and leadership are crucial soft skills to hone, especially to be successful as an environmental professional.

I've reframed that.

These skills are key, but very difficult to pin down and define. Having explored the profession for many years, I have distilled the fundamental skills of a sustainability consultant into five practical, learnable skills:

1. **Technical.**

2. **Communication** (which implies listening and speaking).

3. **Selling** (which implies developing skills like assertiveness, influencing, and storytelling).

4. **Project and People Management.**

5. **Resilience.**

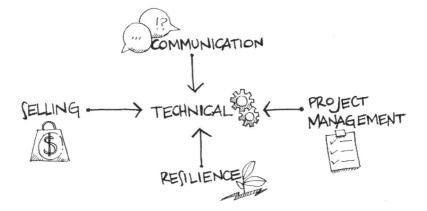

They should all work together harmoniously. Whilst communication is, in my view, the most important starting point, they build and feed on each other.

Let's evaluate them one by one.

CHAPTER 1

How Your Technical Skills Can Support You Throughout Your Career

For most sustainability professionals out there, technical knowledge is the backbone; the base upon which their whole career grows. And whilst you can pull expertise into the projects you're working on, it's still crucial to own and constantly develop a wide base of technical knowledge on sustainability.

Why am I covering this here? To clarify how to care for your technical knowledge, so that it supports you throughout your career.

Imagine your technical knowledge and skills as the foundations upon which you build your profession. At the same time, they give you the direction of your career. If you are an expert in sustainable materials, or circular economy, or ethical fashion, you'll need to spend ample time studying the subject - both formally and informally. You should feel confident in what you know, and, hopefully, begin working at least part of that knowledge in your day-to-day job. That is, if you haven't already.

With a good foundation, right now, you have the skills to advise people, build products, or contribute to sustainability in some shape or form.

However, the foundation of this building is not the building. I bet that you weren't the only student in your course. Right now, there are other people who have studied with you and are trying to make a living with exactly the same tools that you've acquired. There are also many others who've completed a similar course, or maybe two.

So then, what makes YOU different?

Ask yourself this question and consider it for a few minutes. How are you different from your peers? In an interview, going toe-to-toe with someone else, why would a company choose you over that other person?

The answer will vary. It could be your experience; you've worked in the field for a couple years, and have learnt how to apply the theory in practice. This alone makes a huge difference, of course. Between "saying" and "doing" there is a sea, as we say in Italy.

However, even if you are absolutely brilliant at applying your technical skills, there may be others like you who can do the same. Sustainability is becoming mainstream; an opportunity and a passion for many.

You may not have experience yet. So, what can you bring to the table that's different?

Values and Strengths

Start with better understanding your values and strengths. This is something I always coach my clients to do.

You can evaluate what you bring to the table by appreciating and counting on qualities that are unlikely to swing during your career, such as stable traits of your personality, your own personal values, and your strengths. These will support your technical skills.

Check the Action Steps in the downloadable Workbook[22] for tests available online, which you can use to explore your strengths and values, and build your full profile.

Your *values* reflect what is important to you. They are a shorthand way of describing your individual motivations. Together with your beliefs, they are instrumental factors that drive your decision-making. Values are deeply ingrained into who we are and things we wouldn't compromise on, like always being honest, giving priority to your family or the environment, valuing teamwork, or creating a safe and supportive environment.

On the other hand, you may be passionate about teaching others or volunteering. You might love to learn, or have an eye for details. You may have a strategic mind, leadership in your blood, or have a talent for numbers. You might love being at the life and soul of the party, or you may prefer to wonder and reflect before making a decision.

All of these are *character strengths* that can bring a whole new dimension to your professional profile. They can make you the perfect fit for a job, much better than someone else with exactly the same CV.

Your Knowledge as an Evolving Asset

You may have already realised that earning a Master's in sustainability won't make a defining difference in your long-term career. Of course, it might be the start of a bright and successful career, and it's a qualification that makes you eligible to compete in the marketplace - but it's not everything. Even if you've learnt a great deal throughout your university years, knowledge is not a static commodity. You will need to keep up with new theories, new technologies, and new findings, especially in a technical field.

I completed my MSc in 2006 and, at that time in the U.K., the payback for solar panels was close to 100 years. Now, it's between a fifth and a fourth of that. Tomorrow? A completely new solar product may enter the market, one that's very economical to produce and far more efficient in converting sunlight into electricity. It will likely be a film that you can apply onto windows and surfaces to produce energy anywhere, cheaply and conveniently, and the pay-

---

back will be so much shorter. If I only relied on my knowledge of solar panel efficiency from 15 years ago, I would give very incorrect advice to my clients.

Your technical knowledge may be the foundation of your career, but it needs to be kept up-to-date.

Check out the Action Steps in your Workbook for some suggestions on how to do that.

Seeing Value Where Others See Waste

I came across Tiziana Monterisi on LinkedIn. You know how sometimes in life, your destiny is in your name? She has 'risi' in her name, which is the plural of "rice" in Italian. That sparkled my curiosity for her invention, RiceHouse.

On LinkedIn she posted about using rice husks, a waste product that cannot be used for any agricultural or farming purposes (besides poultry), to make natural construction products. Italy produces the most rice in Europe, and the amount of unusable waste created from it is remarkable.

Tiziana is a curious Italian architect, who has spotted an opportunity where others saw rubbish. Tiziana's company, RiceHouse, now produces natural, rice husk construction products, which have high thermal and acoustic insulation with remarkable hygrothermal properties and low VOCs. Her team has built entire houses using these materials.

Tiziana's example is significant because she could have just designed buildings, like thousands of other architects - but she was curious. She observed how, around her home, nature transformed the landscape on a cyclical pattern. She lives in Biella, Italy, where rice is produced, so the landscape goes from brown in winter, to lake-like in spring, to green-yellow in summer, when the rice is harvested. That got her thinking about how buildings should also come from nature, and support human functions as a 'third skin' for us. When she explored how rice is made, she uncovered her opportunity right there.

In order to excel and differentiate yourself from others, you need to stay curious.

Speak to people, watch the world around you with fresh eyes, think about how there's always a different interpretation of the same issue, and a new solution that you might not have spotted before.

Key Points to Remember

Feel free to use this space for jotting down notes on your personal takeaways from this section.

CHAPTER 2

The Power of Communication

*"The single biggest problem in communication is the illusion
that it has taken place."*
-George Bernard Shaw

By now, you have the gist: your technical knowledge will not set you apart from your colleagues or competitors.

So, what will?

I know; you studied for "X" number of years. You've spent ample time, effort, and money in earning those golden-lined certificates that now stare at you from the wall. But I'm afraid those were just your starting points. Those allow you to now call yourself a sustainability professional, and you now have the knowledge to make a process or product more sustainable.

But that doesn't mean you know how to convey the sustainability message to your stakeholder, client, design team, or colleagues. It won't guarantee you a happy client, one that will recommend you to others. It won't guarantee that you deliver the best and most sustainable product or process, either.

But why not?

For a start, you might fail to actively listen to your clients or colleagues, or understand exactly what their specific issue is. It's interesting how we often think that, just because we open our mouth and say stuff, and the other person in front of us does the same, we have communicated. Then, we walk away and can't recall a word of what has been said. Nothing changes as a consequence.

Communication is a two-way street. People forget that. They prioritise delivering a quality presentation in front of a room of board members. Sure, that's very helpful. Being able to stand tall and work through your nerves to clearly explain your ideas will definitely help your career and mission. In fact, presentation skills is a subject that we teach as part of the Green Gorilla Masterclass Programme. But, even for great presenters, it happens time and time again: they don't communicate well.

Once, many years ago, I was invited to an interview for an Associate Director position. The job looked good, so I was excited for the opportunity. Now, you might not believe me when I tell you, but it was the most bizarre interview ever. In fact, it looked like a prank.

My interviewer was the director of the department. She sat down next to me (implying she was friendly, I assume) and started discussing how great the work they conducted there was. She started naming all her clients, all the projects, all high-profile energy companies, all household names. How many millions they were worth, how she managed to land them, and how she had been successful at landing so many jobs over the years because of her skill set. She explained that the Associate Director would need to shadow her, manage all these projects, and hit the ground running, because they had so many fantastic projects that brought hundreds of thousands of pounds to the company…

She talked like a flooding river for half an hour.

She didn't ask me a single question.

Then, she looked at the clock and cheerfully said, "Oh, I have another meeting! Great talking with you. I'll be in touch."

Talking? I felt like I had cobwebs in my mouth… I'm sure it won't surprise you that I didn't accept the job that – even more bizarrely – was offered to me.

Why is it so hard to communicate well?

Some of the reasons are down to the individuals. Influencing factors could be your upbringing; your personal experiences; the place you come from and your culture; your education; your values and biased views; your emotional make-up; and, of course, your character.

Other influencing factors can be down to the environment in which the discussion takes place: over the phone with a cracking line; or in a café, with noise and people around; or perhaps at a bad time, when the other person just received bad news; or, finally, you might speak to a biased audience who's less open to listening.

The two main elements of communication are obviously listening and speaking, but there are also another, equally important component to evaluate: body language.

Let's look at all of them one by one.

Are You *Really* Listening?

The first key to winning over a client (or anyone else we need to work with) is being able to understand their needs. The main way to accomplish this is by actively listening to them.

When you do, you will also tap into extra benefits, such as:

- ◆ If you show your client that you're able to listen attentively, they will open up and trust you more implicitly.

- ◆ Quoting the Dalai Lama: "*When you talk, you are only repeating what you already know. But if you listen, you may learn something new*".

- ◆ You will develop your attention span and patience, skills which come in very little packages these days! Although the jury is still out on whether people's attention spans are shrinking (it could, instead, be a case of ample stimuli competing for our attention, and that we've become faster at digesting information), we *expect* media and people to deliver content more quickly than before. We lose interest almost immediately if our interlocutor doesn't get to the point soon enough.

- ◆ Active listening makes you more approachable, so people are happier to communicate with you.

- ◆ It increases your competence and knowledge, because you can obtain the information you need in an efficient manner. Therefore, you're more likely to complete your tasks successfully.

- ◆ It reduces the chances of misunderstandings and mistakes, therefore saving time and money otherwise spent redoing work.

- ◆ It helps you spot potential issues and risks.

During the interview I mentioned earlier with Jerry Yudelson for Green Gorilla Conversations, he reminded me that God gave us two ears and one mouth, to be used in that proportion. At times, we seem to forget that. Author Steven Covey is quoted saying: *"People don't listen to understand; they listen to reply."*

There is a wonderful TED Talk by Celeste Headlee called "10 Ways to Have a Better Conversation"[23] that I absolutely love, and it opened my own eyes when I first watched it.

Headlee explains that the number-one rule in conversation is to avoid multitasking at all costs. That implies putting down your phone, laptop, or tablet, but also being present. "Be in that moment. Don't think about the argument you had with your boss. Don't think about what you're going to have for dinner. If you want to get out of the conversation, get out of the conversation, but don't be half in it and half out of it."

Another good suggestion is to use open-ended questions: who, what, where, when, and (specifically in our profession) why, as we will see later. By doing so, you'll obtain a far more descriptive answer than "yes" or "no" and gain more insight.

Once you've done this, really listen to the answers. Try and interject as little as possible when others are talking; make a conscious effort to go with the flow of the other person's reasoning; and write down notes, if that helps you cement a few key points to revisit later, instead of interrupting. That also allows you to momentarily 'let go' of that particular point, so you don't play and replay a planned response in your head, making you lose concentration.

---

23 www.ted.com/talks/celeste_headlee_10_ways_to_have_a_better_conversation/

When you pontificate and don't let others speak because you have to show off your knowledge or personal values, you won't get very far in our profession - or in any of your other endeavours, for that matter. It's hard. I know because I used to be a very chatty child and an even chattier adult; when you know your stuff, you want the world to know. You also care deeply about the environment and that radiates from everything you say.

However, your client may not want to save the orangutans. Your client may want to earn a lot of money very quickly instead. They may want to be the first to certify a specific type of building under an environmental label in their country, for marketing purposes. They might need to report back to GRESB, the Environmental and Social Governance Benchmark for Real Estates, whilst driving their SUVs and pumping CO_2 into the atmosphere.

Your job, as an environmental and sustainability professional, is not to judge them on the basis of your different values. Instead, you should listen to their pain, like a confessor would, understand it well, and then respond with a perfectly tailored sustainability solution. Even if they don't share your views, acknowledge their needs and crack on with making a positive change, whilst attending to their requirements.

The Role of Empathy in Good Communication

In fact, in order to truly listen to people and have meaningful conversations, clients or not, you should develop another key skill: *empathy*.

You don't have to believe what they believe, or share their views, but exercising empathy will help you step into the other person's shoes and see where they're coming from. It's not about agreeing; it's about understanding. If you get inside their heads and truly grasp their perspective, you can better communicate with them - and possibly reach an agreement. Psychotherapy research shows that, when individuals feel listened to, they tend to listen to themselves more carefully, evaluating and clarifying their own thoughts or feelings. In other words, when someone feels listened to, they can even change their own mind - without you having to do a single thing.

We Communicate with Our Bodies Too

A huge (and often forgotten) element of communication is body language.

Think about the last time you were uncomfortable in a conversation. How did you feel and how did your body react? Were your arms open and interlocked behind your head? Or were they tucked in between your legs? Did you look the other person in the eye, or did you look down at your hands?

"Open" and "closed" postures are instinctive human behaviours, which can tell whether or not a person is at ease and in control - far better than words can.

There is science behind it all, but it's mostly down to personal interpretation and how the filters of our own experience determine what we see.

Albert Mehrabian is an American psychologist best-known for his publications on the relative importance of verbal and nonverbal messages. According to him, only an average 7% of the true meaning behind a message is down to the words we choose. Around 38% is down to voice and 55% to body language, especially if body language and voice distract the audience for the wrong reasons – such as too loud, too quiet, too jumpy, too rigid, etc. Attention naturally diverts to the element that's at odds with your words.

For example, if someone says, "I don't have a problem with you", but avoids eye contact, looks anxious, or has a trembling voice, you're entitled to think that they indeed have a problem with you.

In general, you can read the person you're listening to by looking at their body language and facial expressions. From it, you can glean valuable information about their emotions and the reliability of their words. Likewise, by understanding your own instinctive body language and how to consciously use it, you can create rapport. That's an essential skill to master.

Yes, body language is as complex and multifaceted as a spoken language and will require a long time to grasp fully. However, it's useful to adopt even the basic elements, so you can try to better understand your audience and create immediate rapport.

Where do you start? Let's explore the basics.

Open and Closed Postures

An open posture (open arms, feet firmly on the ground, legs shoulder-width apart) is perceived as a sign of dominance and self-assurance. Even just standing up tall, with your shoulders back (like birds puffing up their chests when approaching other birds) can have a similar effect.

A study conducted by University College London, which involved over 2,000 people from Europe, Asia, and America, tested how people of all ages and backgrounds react to different standing positions. The evidence showed that people standing with their feet shoulder-width apart were 32% more likely to gain votes in an election, as compared to people who kept their feet together - even when all other factors were kept the same.

The study also showed that strong gestures were rated as more confident and inspiring, as compared to limp gestures or stillness.

If you want to practise a strong standing position, you can try the yogic Tadasana, or Mountain Pose. As a side effect, this pose can help improve posture, balance, and focus.

- Stand with your feet shoulder-width apart.

- Breathe deeply and easily.

- Rock forwards and backwards on the soles of your feet to find the point where your weight is spread evenly over your feet.

- Create a solid base by spreading your toes and firmly gripping the floor.

- Tuck in your tailbone slightly.

- Elongate your body and broaden your collarbone.

- Keep your arms straight along your trunk, fingers extended.

- Elongate your neck and head.

The easiest way to remember good posture in this pose? Imagine a cord coming up from the top of your skull, gently pulling the crown of your head upwards.

Now, think about a time when you talked to someone who didn't agree with you. Perhaps they had their arms folded in front of their body, they had a minimal or tense facial expression, or they avoided eye contact. It probably felt like they created a barricade to hide behind, or that all they wanted was to either attack or dodge you.

That's a classic example of closed posture. In conversation, if you catch someone closing up in a similar way, open up your own posture to show a willingness to collaborate. It might help move on from the issue.

Body Language and Leadership

If you want examples of body language used effectively to communicate, think about great historical leaders well-known for their charisma, professionalism, and ability to create rapport. These are three recognised signs of effective leadership.

Charismatic people are particularly expressive, sensitive, and have strong internal control. They are self-assured and articulated in their point, but they show their leadership mostly through their body language. Imagine a leader that uses open hands gestures, their palms turning upwards and slightly towards their audience. They are inviting, and communicate both openness and a willingness to collaborate.

Now, think about a leader who has great internal control, but is rigid in their gestures, doesn't show any empathy, and doesn't try to create rapport. Someone who speaks by pointing their index finger at the audience, keeping their hands on their hips, leaving their palms face-down, and using strong hand gestures, like one hand "chopping" the other.

They come across as cold, domineering, and arrogant. I'm sure you can think of at least one right now!

First Steps Towards Mastering Your Body Language to Improve Communication

Next time you're in a meeting, check your posture. At the very minimum, straighten up.

Someone once told me, "The best piece of advice I received in my early career was: even as an intern, don't be the one who takes the notes in meetings.

It makes you lower your head and assume a submissive posture. That sends a message to the room about who is lowest in the ranks."

When you genuinely engage and create rapport, you will come across as more confident and likeable. People will open up to you easily.

Relax, smile, and look them in the eye.

An effective technique for creating fast rapport is to mirror the posture of the person in front of you - without making it too obvious, or else they'll feel mocked. For example, if they tilt their head to one side or fold their arms, you can slowly do the same, like you're in front of a mirror. It's called *limbic synchrony* and we all do it in non-conscious ways. We do it when we're talking with someone we like, are interested in, or agree with, signalling that we are connected and engaged. It's a proven method to show empathy.

At the bare minimum, treat people with respect, avoid aggressive gestures, and watch the magic happen.

How to Speak with Impact

Within the first couple months of the Green Gorilla's journey, whilst I was developing courses for sustainability professionals, I had an epiphany: to really create a better world, the sustainability message needs to be passed on to children.

I volunteered to bring sustainability to my local school. During their assemblies, I spoke to the children about energy, climate change, and waste. Would you believe that these were some of the toughest presentations I've ever delivered? Can you explain to a six-year-old what climate change is, how it's happening, and what the consequences are – all without using jargon or scaring them?

That experience made me heavily reflect about jargon, and the need to simplify our message if we want that message to get far. I had to unpack all the knowledge in my head, step back, and reformulate: climate change, carbon emissions, greenhouse gases, renewable energy. Even these terms, which are more or less household words to the majority of adults, have absolutely no meaning to a child.

Even if you don't speak to children about sustainability and environmental matters, think about how much a client can actually get from your message. You need to be ready to explain complex concepts in a more palatable, simple-to-understand way.

Of course, it's a fine balance between helping your client and patronising them. If you tune into their facial expressions and ask the right questions, you can better understand if your client has any knowledge of the subject or not. To err on the side of caution, use plain language.

Steve Jobs was a master storyteller and presenter. His keynotes to introduce new Apple products were pretty legendary, and you may have seen the videos. In 2007, Jobs introduced the iPhone at the Macworld conference. Whilst talking about the iPhone's music features, he could have used terms like:

- Control your music through innovative touch sensitive controls.

- Widescreen 16:9 aspect ratio video playback.

- High resolution 153pp graphics...

...and the like.

After all, he was speaking to a crowd of adults - and, what's more, Apple enthusiasts. Most would have understood. But not *everyone*.

Instead, on the giant screen behind him, there were the following bullet points:

- Touch your music.

- Widescreen video.

- Find your music even faster.

- Gorgeous album art.

- Built-in speaker.

- Cover flow.

His plain language could be understood by elementary school children. His message was memorable because it was purposefully simple. As such, it went very, very far.

Steve Jobs did not trivialise technology. Quite the opposite, he made it accessible by ensuring it was smart and simple to use at the same time, and his language perfectly reflects his company's ethos.

Now ask yourself:

- In a meeting, do you feel compelled to show your expertise and technical knowledge by using technical terms?

- Do you feel your clients would think less of you if you didn't use jargon or a few percentages and data?

- Are you too eager to get on with the nitty-gritty of the work, and often forget the big picture, the reason, and the vision?

If Steve Jobs could use plain language and captivate audiences with his amazing vision and plain language, what's stopping you from doing the same?

Therefore, it's crucial to look for jargon when speaking to people. Use the checklist in the recap paragraph at the end of this chapter to ensure the language you use is simple enough for your clients and other non-technical people.

Aside from that, consider the content of your pitch when you speak to a client. I'll go into more detail when I cover selling, but the key to a successful pitch is to understand who you have in front of you, what's important for them, what their "why" and needs are, and flex your pitch to adapt. In the Steve Jobs example, he clearly sold the benefits of the iPhone, not its features. That's what his audience cared about; that's what was in it for them. Ask yourself whether you sell the features of sustainability, or its benefits.

The way you deliver your pitch can enlighten, inspire, scare, illustrate, educate, or excite people. The different influencing and storytelling techniques you leverage will depend on the situation, the person in front of you, and what's important to them.

I suggest evaluating the pitch you generally use with clients, as well as any standard sustainability explanation or introduction you currently use.

Do you always use the same words and examples, no matter who's in front of you? To practise adapting to different audiences and explaining technical subjects, try delivering them to your family or friends and see if they understand you. Can you convince or inspire them to buy into your ideas by using language they can understand, different examples they might be familiar with, or by flexing your style?

Use Your Voice as a Tool to Communicate Effectively

The voice is a magnificent musical instrument, one we often think comes with the package and cannot be changed much. But, of course, actors and singers spend years adjusting it, modulating it, caring for it as one of their most precious assets.

Even if you don't want to take singing or acting lessons, you can definitely pay attention to the way you use your voice, its pitch, and its rhythm – such as the pauses you use, which can be as powerful as the words you say. From the sound of your voice, your listeners will make judgments about your attitude towards them and the ideas you're presenting. They'll judge your sincerity and credibility, in part, by your voice. In turn, that will affect how they respond to you and your message.

I'm sure you've attended a presentation that was delivered at a very low-volume or monotone voice. What did that tell you about the person? It may suggest that they don't care much about their listeners; they're here to deliver the presentation and shoot off to their next meeting. Without any emphasis on certain words, you struggle to understand the most important parts of their speech.

I love this example of how, depending on the word you emphasise and how intonation is used, you provide a completely different meaning to the phrase:

"*I* didn't tell her you were stupid." *(Somebody else told her.)*

"I *didn't* tell her you were stupid." *(I emphatically did not.)*

"I didn't *tell* her you were stupid." *(I implied it.)*

"I didn't tell *her* you were stupid." *(I told someone else.)*

"I didn't tell her *you* were stupid." *(I told her someone else was stupid.)*

"I didn't tell her you *were* stupid." *(I told her you're still stupid.)*

"I didn't tell her you were *stupid*." *(I told her something else about you.)*

How powerful is our voice? Seven different meanings; exactly the same phrase.

Quickening and slowing down also creates pacing; slow down to emphasise and draw attention to an idea. Speak too quickly, and you communicate that you are nervous and lack confidence.

How about the volume of your voice and its timber?

Speak too loudly and you send a message that you're aggressive and overpowering. However, use your voice firmly and at a volume that can be heard by everyone in the room, and you show confidence.

Let's Recap: How to Communicate Effectively

Listening

Next time you're in a conversation with someone, try to practice some active listening.

- Face the speaker and maintain eye contact, putting aside any distracting thoughts (as much as possible). A few suggestions for this include:

  - When you realise you're ruminating or lost in thought, try labelling your distraction. For example, as "thought" or "feeling", without judging yourself for having lost concentration. This simple mindfulness technique will gently acknowledge your thoughts and bring you back to the room.

  - If the thought concerns an important topic you mustn't forget, just write it down and come back to the person in front of you.

  - If your mobile phone or emails are distracting you, agree on a tech-free meeting when possible; put your mobiles and laptops away and focus entirely on the meeting.

- Ask open questions. Listen intently to the answer, without interrupting, until there is a natural pause in the other person's flow.

- Pay attention to the person you're speaking to from the start. They might be making small talk, and perhaps ask or say things that are of interest to them. They may be talking about family, pets, or travelling… Keep a mental note of what they care about outside of the business conversation; these are clues to their values. When it's your turn to speak, you can reframe your offer around their needs, but also around things they value.

- Practise your empathy. Try listening to understand, and suspend judgement for a minute. Just let the other person's reasons sink in before formulating your reply. Listen without judging the speaker and without jumping to conclusions; this would only stop you from listening attentively until they have finished expressing their thoughts. It may help to jot down a quick note and remind yourself of that particular conversation item at the end of their speech, so you can return and ask further questions if needed. Once noted down, go back to actively listening.

- At the end, ask yourself how it went. Did you feel anxious? Did you feel the urge to interrupt? Did you gain more insight than usual? What would you do differently next time?

Speaking

Jargon:

- What words do you use that your friends and relatives would not understand?

    - Too long / too technical? (e.g. Rematerialisation, Interoperability, Biomimicry, Biophilic, etc.).

    - Acronyms (e.g. CSR, ESG, HVAC, EMS, etc.)?

    - Expressions (e.g. value proposition, carbon footprint, circular economy, cradle to grave, etc.).

- Is there alternative wording you can use instead?

- If you MUST use that word or expression, what's a clear and memorable way to explain it?

Voice:

When speaking, be sure that:

- You have the right pitch, volume, and speed (think about whether you need to adjust the dial of any of these three).

- You are expressive. Think about someone who has a monotone expression or, on the other hand, who over-modulates their voice to the point of annoyance. You don't want to come across like Dory from Finding Nemo, speaking whale! Place yourself in the middle.

- You breathe deeply. Shallow breathing doesn't allow your voice to fully project. You could try this exercise:

- Relax your stomach muscles.

- Breathe in through your nose and fill up your abdomen first, then your lower ribs (you should feel them expand) and then all the way up to your chin.

- Hold this breath for a count of ten.

- Now exhale slowly. As you exhale, keep your ribs expanded and tighten your abdomen as you would during a "crunch"—that is, the lower abdominal muscles should come in first.

- Repeat. Once you have mastered the exercise, practise incorporating it into your speaking. This may be done slowly at first, until you can coordinate all the actions smoothly.

- It's crucial that your breathing is low and expansive. If you perform the exercise correctly, your stomach will go in, whilst your chest will stay out and expand. Practising this technique will provide many benefits, including:

  - Reduced fatigue during and after your speech.

  - Proper posture for breathing creates a confident, strong appearance. Deeper breathing makes you feel more confident and stronger.

  - Deep breathing reduces tension and helps to focus intellectual activity.

- You take pauses. Pauses are as important as your voice. The right pauses create gravitas and enrich what you're saying. Don't rush your words, as this translates as a sign of insecurity. Instead, take your time so that you establish your presence in the room.

Body Language:

Fundamental body language to practise includes:

- Make eye contact.

- Smile genuinely (more on this in the *Selling 101* chapter).

- Keep your head high.

- Stand tall, with feet firmly on the ground and legs shoulder-width apart. Do you feel different than when you stand in a less balanced way?

- Arms and legs are uncrossed.

- Have a firm handshake.

Key Points to Remember

Feel free to use this space for jotting down notes on your personal takeaways from this section.

CHAPTER 3

Selling 101 for Technical People

I bet when I say the word "selling", most of you have an immediate reaction:

"Selling? Me? I can't do that! I'm a technical person! I can talk to you about sustainable urban drainage systems all day long, but selling? No, that's not for me."

I also bet, when you hear that word, you're picturing something like this:

Well, let me tell you: we *all* sell, not just the professional salespeople.[24] Of course, we don't always exchange money, but we influence people to move them towards our goals - all the time, consciously or not.

A simple example is when we convince our children to have one more bite of their dinner. We're in fact *selling it* to them, by explaining the benefits of doing it ("You're going to grow strong"), and the consequences of not doing it ("You won't have pudding at the end"). Perhaps, we even use their emotions to win them over ("Mummy will be sad if you don't"), or diverting their attention ("Look at that aeroplane carrying your broccoli!"). These are all techniques used in selling.

In today's world, more of us are asked to influence others or make an actual sale, even when it's not our job. In most companies, everyone, even admin staff, is deemed responsible for selling the services that the company provides.

---

24 Author Daniel Pink describes this well in *To Sell is Human*. A great read for 'accidental' sales people. D.H. Pink, *To Sell is Human*, Riverhead Books, 2012

Think about the cashier at the newsagent, asking if you need any chocolate or batteries whilst you're paying for a magazine.

But particularly in our field, being able to 'sell' sustainability is just as important as knowing the technical details of how a building can be made more energy efficient. You will never reach those details if you can't sell the big picture to your stakeholders first.

The good news is? You don't have to be a sly used-car salesman, even if you associate that with selling.

When I was in my 20s, on my way home from work, I occasionally stopped to have a look at the shopping mall. This one time, I didn't really need anything, but I was browsing clothes and makeup. A male promoter was behind the counter at one of the big makeup brands. He wasn't polished and well-suited; he had long, wavy hair in a ponytail, and he was dressed in jeans and a jumper. I found it slightly odd that a man, especially clothed in that way, was selling makeup; he was actually selling a small kit to make nails look shiny without nail polish.

I pretended I wasn't looking – you know that if you engage with a salesperson, they're going to get you. But then he made a joke. I laughed, and before I could do anything else, he was already showing me how the main item of that kit, a small buffer, worked. As a result, his nails looked really shiny, to my surprise. He presented the included travel bag; talked about how wonderful my hands would look, naturally, just by using this kit; how I would save money by not buying nail polish; threw in a tiny bottle of cuticle oil and a cheap, scented hand cream 'for free'.... and, tah-dah, I was at the till, paying £20 (down from £30, of course, just because it was me).

Whilst I forked out a £20 note (20 years ago, that was some money) for four tiny pieces of foam board (like the kind we used at university to make architectural models), a tiny cuticle oil bottle, and a cheap hand cream, I felt gobsmacked. He'd been so charming and smart; had he been selling dog poop in nicely packaged pink boxes, I would've bought it.

I had to tell him: "You are a fantastic salesman."

But how had he convinced me to buy something of obvious poor quality, that I didn't need, and at an extortionate price?

The lesson that young salesman gave me went far beyond teaching me that I am naïve and gullible.

He showed me that selling is not some magical hormone you either have or don't have. You can actually learn it, by putting together a few fundamental elements.

I reflected on this episode many times afterwards, and I concluded that he possessed a very well-honed script. He created rapport first, engaging with me by cracking a joke. Then he immediately displayed what was in it for me; he showed the results of using the kit, without focusing on the details of the kit itself. By throwing in stuff for 'free', he seemed generous and made me feel unique. He looked down to earth and friendly.

He didn't do everything right – but I was young and easy prey.

Now I deplore that he effectively conned me into a deal that wasn't worth the money. I used that kit three times in total, although I kept the foam boards until recently, just to remind myself that I'm not so smart after all.

A good salesman's first and most important skill is to be able to listen.

We talked about listening in the previous chapter, but it's worth stressing here: to move others, you must first prioritise listening. That young chap didn't even ask me what I was looking for, or whether I needed nail polish, or if I liked grooming my nails, or whatever else actually concerned *me*. He was probably scared of a negative response, so his approach was to launch into selling mode.

Yes, he did sell the kit to me, but the magic bubble burst at the checkout, and I immediately regretted my purchase. I wouldn't have bought his product a second time, so ethical selling and attending to your client's needs is fundamental for repeated business, and to be recommended to others.

Had he matched my needs with the product he was selling, I would've been far happier. Most likely, I wouldn't have remembered this episode for the wrong reasons 20 years later.

Let me tell you another example, closer to us, in the sustainability world.

When I worked as a Business Developer Manager for the BRE Innovation Park, I had great fun meeting wacky inventors. They often had mind-blowing ideas and technologies that went beyond anything I'd seen before, all of which addressed sustainability issues in a bold, brave, and wonderful way.

But… some of them weren't good communicators. They were the classic types who would wear a Christmas jumper in August under their white coat. They loved building stuff in their garden shed, but didn't have a clue about how to explain those inventions to the wider public and sell the benefits to potential clients.

Once, this small, wonderful company arrived to pitch their invention at the Innovation Park. Their key product were these amazing, solar-heating roof tiles, which looked like ordinary tiles, but would extract and store heat from the outdoors to use inside buildings, even when temperatures outside were as low as -7 °C.

There you go ,I've explained it to you in 30 words.

The engineer behind the invention sat us down for one and a half hours, trying to explain his invention in great detail ,talking about how it worked using technical jargon - acronyms and all .And not a single diagram.

He was obviously a genius with no commercial acumen whatsoever (I'm pleased to say that, last time I checked, the company had a smart website with a video animation to *show* you how the system operates, using graphics and only a few simple words).

The thing is, that brilliant engineer didn't step into his potential customer's shoes. He jumped into explaining the system's characteristics with jargon and his technical knowledge, which was *his* language and not ours.

He *assumed* we knew what he was talking about. But he never checked - not once in the excruciating one-and-a-half hour presentation he gave, which we spent utterly confused.

It's important to understand that, by using simple language, you are not trivialising science (I will explain more in the Storytelling section). You are making your ideas and services accessible (and sellable!) to others, who may lack your technical knowledge or need your help navigating the complex world of sustainability.

Now, let's look at the *ideal* selling process and skills needed for us sustainability professionals.

1. Change the Way You See Yourself.

If you're interested in becoming a better 'accidental' salesperson, read Daniel Pink's *To Sell is Human*. The concept that most resonated with me from the book is that salespeople (accidental or not) don't need to con people into buying something they don't need or want.

The most effective salesperson is a curator of the abundant information available out there.

Gone are the days of salespeople being the only experts, using that expertise against clueless buyers. Often you'll find that clients, especially those in our sector, have gone through a number of sustainability projects themselves; they may know more than you on certain aspects of sustainability.

The internet has opened up infinite opportunities for people to educate themselves and become more conscious buyers in any field, including product specifications, sustainability services, and technologies. However, it's no different than being at the British Library without a librarian or a catalogue to tell you where to look.

So your role, as a salesperson who has technical expertise, is to guide people through the ocean of information available. You should clarify that information and develop a plan for your clients to follow.

You're there to serve people and not to scam them. In most cases, they probably approached you; they want you to be their guide. So do it. It's ethical and it's in line with your values.

In order to influence others, and communicate the sustainability message so that people understand it, you need to change the way you see yourself.

Elisabetta was one of the first sustainability professionals to train with Green Gorilla. She had extensive knowledge of sustainability through many years of study and work in the sector, specifically advising designers on the implementation of sustainable lighting. Before coming across Green Gorilla, Elisabetta focused 100% of her attention on acquiring more technical knowledge, and she didn't see herself as a leader.

She felt she lacked the confidence to convince design teams to adopt her solutions. So, she enrolled in the Green Gorilla Masterclass Programme to learn more about the business case for sustainability, as well as the techniques to bring that content alive.

The training made her realise that the method of delivering your message (the "HOW") is as important as the actual message (the "WHAT"), especially if you aim to sway people's decisions towards your goals.

At some point in your career, you may need to influence people you have no control over. For example, when you're an external consultant working with a company that is not yours, or if you're in a junior role and don't have formal authority over the people you work with.

The best way to exercise your authority, when you don't technically have authority, is to boost your so-called 'controlled, high presence', assertive persona. People with high presence look confident and comfortable, speak clearly and persuasively, and think clearly even under pressure. They act with intention. They are in touch with and in control of their emotions.

This doesn't mean being aggressive, controlling, or overwhelming, but rather, shifting your mind-set to:

- Thinking that you, and your opinions, matter.

- Being assertive.

- Being proactive.

- Being measured.

The likely outcome is that your attitude will shift how you are perceived by others. You will come across as interesting and worth listening to.

Why? Because an assertive person operates from a place of equality and respect, not of superiority or inferiority. This will give others confidence that you know what you're talking about and that you won't impose on them something against their interests. Your opinions will be more respected because you will respect others' opinions.

The first step to boosting your high persona and assertiveness is to identify your limiting beliefs (i.e. those that constrain your potential). This specifically regards who you are and who you aren't, which you'll need to change into positive propositions.

Limiting beliefs tend to appear in our minds as:

- Excuses.

- Negative thoughts.

- Justifications.

- Worries.

- Beliefs conditioned from culture or family.

- Thought patterns.

- Perfectionistic thinking.

- Past failures.

- Fear.

If you experience dissatisfaction at work and are not actively changing the situation, chances are, you have limiting beliefs holding you back.

By using the exercise in the Action Steps in the downloadable Workbook, explore what untrue beliefs are withholding your true potential.

Once you've identified your limiting beliefs, rewrite them in a positive, proactive, and actionable way.

For example:

If you feel your knowledge is insufficient, you're not good enough for this job, or aren't as good as others (which isn't objectively true), write:

- I have studied my whole life and I know what I'm talking about.

If you believe you don't have sufficient experience for this job, you can write:

- I can bring a fresh pair of eyes to this situation, and experience will come in time.

There are areas in your life where preparation and a little research can boost confidence and silence limiting beliefs when you need to perform. For example, if you believe you can't present, try:

- I will prepare and rehearse well before my next presentation.

If you hate networking and think you're awkward in those situations, write:

- In my next networking session, I will research the people that are attending and prepare to speak to three of them who can add value to my life.

Assertiveness (owning your feelings, being clear about the message you want to deliver, and delivering it in a pristine way) goes hand in hand with confidence.

Build Your Confidence

But how do you build confidence?

When approaching your profession, the more you "do", the more confident you will be.

Confidence is built on accomplishment, so the more you accomplish (especially if your goals are in line with your values), the better you'll feel about yourself, and the more your confidence will grow.

> *"Confidence comes not from always being right, but from not fearing to be wrong."*
> -Peter T. Mcintyre, painter and author

At this point, you may ask: *"This is all well and good, but what if I'm new to the profession?"*

I'm sure you recall all the hurdles you've faced to reach this point - personal, emotional, and physical even. Nights spent revising for exams, long commutes, working at minimum wage to pay for your studies, sacrifices by your family to get here...

These are all achievements that we tend to forget once we reach our objectives. And, of course, we want to forget our failures; the times that we misjudged a situation or a person, or the hurt we might've caused.

For guidance on this, I look to David Goggins, a Navy SEAL who served in Iraq and Afghanistan, and an accomplished ultramarathon runner, ultra-distance cyclist, and triathlete. He places all the elements that shaped him (good and bad) in a mental 'cookie jar', which he revisits to remind himself that he's already gone through tough times - and, as such, he can overcome any current difficulty.

Here is what Goggins says about the cookie jar:

> *What do you say to yourself when life is kicking your ass? When you keep failing at the things you truly want? This question was asked of me.*
>
> *I thank God for testing me again.*
>
> *I go back to what I call the cookie jar.*
>
> *Some people try to forget the bad in their life.*
>
> *I use my bad for strength when needed; great lessons learned.*
>
> *In that cookie jar, I pull out whatever I need for the task at hand.*

Use the Action Steps in your Workbook to write your list of "cookies".

The cookie jar method builds upon previous experiences. However, to become more confident, it's just as important to explore the scary, unknown space outside your comfort zone.

How to Overcome Your Fear of Failure

You may experience fear of failure, and that's what undermines your confidence and stops you from being assertive. If that's the case, you're in good company; most people experience fear before attempting actions outside of their comfort zone.

However, be aware that there is no growth inside your comfort zone. You may also later regret your lack of action. I promise you: regret is a much heavier weight to bear than fear.

Psychologist Susan Jeffers says, "*Feel the fear and do it anyway*". You can practise experiencing fear, acknowledging it, and taking action anyway. The more you throw yourself into the deep end, the more manageable it becomes - especially if you focus on the consequences of *not* doing it.

Ask yourself: *what's the worst that can happen?* The stoic Seneca teaches us that "*to reduce your worry, you must assume that what you fear may happen is certainly going to happen.*" You'll likely realise that, even if the worst happens (you stumble on every single word, you trip on a cable and fall face-first on the floor right before the CEO, you make a right dog's dinner of your presentation and everyone laughs wildly… you get the gist), you will still survive.

In the grand scheme of things, this single mishap will not matter. Think about yourself in five or ten years' time. Will this single failure still burn?

Chances are, the worst won't actually happen, but this stoic little mental exercise may help you let go of hesitance and reduce your anxiety.

Admittedly, I'm not naturally good at failing. My perfectionist nature imposes a ridiculously high standard on the quality of my work. Any setback, or delay, or criticism feels like a personal failure to me. In my previous endeavours, I had to learn through losing jobs or being pushed aside by less qualified people that failure is not only normal, but also fundamental to personal growth.

How can we empathise with others if we've never failed? How can we see what opportunities exist outside the little box we shut ourselves in if we don't come out of it? How can we understand our limits and the extent of our ambition if we aren't put to the test?

A brilliant quote I love, which has been attributed to Nelson Mandela, says: *In life, sometimes you win and sometimes you learn.* A bad episode may be necessary to learn a valuable lesson.

Using Visualisation to Increase Your Chances of Success

Because people come in different kinds, shapes, and forms, you may dislike being pessimistic.

There's a great exercise you can try, which is used on a regular basis by many high-performance athletes, from Michael Phelps to Andy Murray. It's to visualise your performance before a big meeting or situation where you have to perform at your best.

Footballer Wayne Rooney has leveraged this technique throughout his life. In interviews, he said that the night before a match, he lies in bed and visualises the match in great detail, trying to recall all the feelings and sensations. When he visualises scoring a goal, he can feel his foot hitting the ball, the smell of grass under his feet, and the sound of the crowd.

This incredibly vivid imagery helps an athlete to prepare mentally, by improving their confidence, focus, clarity, and speed of thought. It helps them prepare for any scenario; how will I react to the crowd? What if we go 1-0 down? What shot will I take in a certain situation? It also fires impulses to the muscles, therefore priming them for action. The more vivid the mental image, the more effectively their brain primes their body to complete the same physical and technical action in a real game.

Sports psychologist Dr. Richard Suinn found that visual rehearsal actually triggers neural firings in the muscles and creates a mental blueprint, which can ultimately facilitate future performance. Using electromyographic equipment, Suinn discovered that skiers who simply visualised skiing downhill fired electrical impulses and produced muscle patterns almost identical to those found when the skiers actually hit the slopes. Of course, no amount of visualisation can make up for years of physical practice. However, it seems that mental rehearsal can, indeed, help an athlete to fire up their body for optimal performance.

Tennis player Andy Murray has been known to make several visits to a deserted Centre Court in advance of Wimbledon, so as to mentally acclimatise to the environment.

You could do the same. Try and imagine your next meeting in as much detail as you can. What will success look like for you? In the visualisation, include what you'll wear, the facial expressions of the people sitting there, the smell of coffee in the background, the whirring sound of the projector, and so on. If you can, be like Murray and go visit the venue when nobody is there, so you can grow familiar with the environment beforehand.

Alternatively, use a mix of the techniques above. A controlled mixture of pessimism and optimism can lead you to grow more efficiently.

Practise Being a Green Gorilla

If you want to be viewed as confident – and, therefore, have a higher chance of influencing others - you need to control the use of your voice and your body language, as explained in the chapter about speaking.

If you don't feel confident before meetings and presentations, you can try quickly boosting your levels of testosterone (which increases confidence), whilst decreasing your levels of cortisol (which is linked to stress and anxiety). There is a great little exercise that can help empower you before meetings or important conversations. It's called Power Posing. This technique has been discussed heavily, and if you want the science behind it, you can watch Amy Cuddy's TED talk.[25]

Find yourself a toilet or empty room (you don't want to look like a fool in front of others, presumably). Then, stand tall in an open posture, legs shoulder-width apart, with your chest out and your hands on your hips (think Wonder Woman). Research shows that standing like this for a couple of minutes increases your levels of testosterone and decreases your cortisol, providing the quick confidence boost you need. If you don't feel like doing the pose, or you can't for any reason, it has been demonstrated that even visualising a powerful pose in your head can increase your power and self-confidence.

25 www.ted.com/talks/amy_cuddy_your_body_language_may_shape_who_ you_are

Olivia Fox Cabane in her book *The Charisma Myth* suggests that you visualise yourself walking into the meeting room as a big (green!) gorilla. Imagine taking up as much space as possible, puffing up your chest, and broadening your shoulders. Focus on your breath and the feelings of power this pose gives you.

In these situations, breath is a second ally of yours.

Aside from the exercise discussed in the *Speaking* section about using your voice as a powerful instrument, there are several calming breathing techniques out there. You don't need to go full yogi before a presentation (but do, if it helps!). Just breathing consciously, using the "4-7-8 technique", will help:

♦ Exhale completely through your mouth, making a whoosh sound.

♦ Close your mouth and inhale quietly through your nose to a mental count of four.

♦ Hold your breath for a count of seven.

♦ Exhale completely through your mouth, making a whoosh sound to a count of eight.

♦ Repeat it a few times, and you'll feel your anxiety magically drop.

Finally, you can try exercises to release tension.

For the first technique, "shake" your body (especially the parts that feel more tense, like your arms and shoulders), and jump up and down (letting out any sounds too, if that feels good). Listen to your body and take it easy if you have an injury.

The second is a Qigong-based exercise, called "tapping". It works similarly to acupuncture (but without needles) to stimulate vital body points. It consists of tapping (as lightly or vigorously as you please) your eyebrow area, temples, crown of your head, arms, chest, kidney area, and legs, using the tips of your fingers to reactivate blood flow, increase energy, and release tension.

Once you've controlled your nerves and are before an audience, there are several influencing techniques you can use, depending on the people in front of you. Being able to flex your style according to who you're addressing is a great skill that you can perfect to better ensure future success.

2. Do Your Research

To gain your audiences' favour, the first step is to know them. There is a plethora of information already at your fingertips, and it's wise to approach a new client after having researched a portion of their sustainability stance beforehand.

Corporate Development Stage

Whilst conducting research for this book, I came across this excellent parallel between the well-known Maslow's hierarchy of human needs, and business needs created by B2B International.[26]

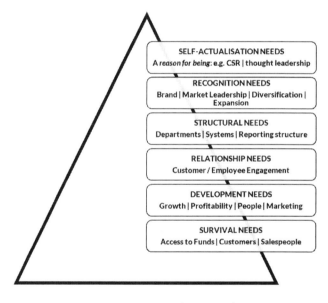

Business needs pyramid

Any business you come across, at different stages of their development, will have some needs to be fulfilled - very similarly to human beings. Certain needs will pertain to their stage and evolve with time, while others will stay constant as the company grows. I recommend getting familiar with this "need" pyra-

---

26 www.b2binternational.com/publications/introducing-the-business-to-business-hierarchy-of-needs/

mid, as it will help you ask your clients the right questions, depending on where they're at.

Sustainability Journey

There is another useful model, developed by the Doughty Centre for Corporate Responsibility at Cranfield University[27], which defines a business's current and desired stages of corporate responsibility:

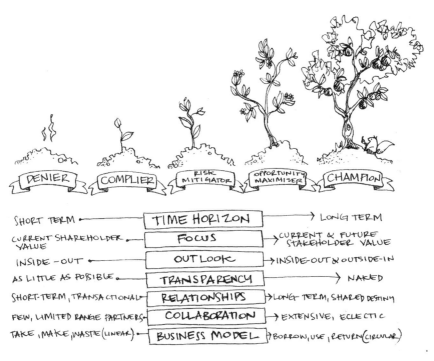

Maturity levels can help organisations (and consultants) understand where they currently stand. Furthermore, it can stimulate creative thinking about potential solutions for how to reach the next level. The maturity level of a company influences their business purpose, strategy, organisation, policies, practices, and performance.

---

27   www.cranfield.ac.uk/som/research-centres/doughty-centre-for-corporate-responsibility/stages-of-corporate-maturity

If their journey towards sustainability is not evident from the company's website, sustainability annual report, and social media, this could be a subject to cover in the first meeting.

Sustainability Drivers

Next, you should identify the company's main drivers for seeking sustainability. Drivers at a corporate level generally fall within these five categories:

- ◆ Client expectations.

- ◆ Improve and maintain reputation.

- ◆ Transform business over time.

- ◆ Legal compliance.

- ◆ Values-based response to minimise impacts[28].

Understanding their drivers is important, because any decision your client makes will be in line with those. That's their "why".

Barriers to Sustainability Adoption

Finally, it's wise to understand potential barriers you'll encounter when implementing sustainability within the organisation, such as:

- ◆ Financial.

- ◆ General business culture.

- ◆ Lack of clear strategic or operational alignment.

- ◆ Lack of management support.

- ◆ Direct resistance to change.

Be aware that the barriers may be less obvious; you won't find this information on their website, for sure! It may require some investigation. Once you

---

28 www.iema.net/reading-room/2016/11/30/beyond-the-perfect-storm-(2016)

uncover it, however, it will help you tune-in to their needs and aspirations, and pitch sustainability at the right level.

3. Build Personal Rapport

Getting to know your client is important. Any successful relationship starts with taking an interest in the other person. Saying something meaningful is much better than total silence after having talked about the weather and how your journey was. This can be done by investing time to research the actual person you'll meet beforehand.

It takes five minutes to look at their company's About Us page on their website, but also at their LinkedIn profile; see whether there are special interests in their history of employment, schools, or voluntary activities that can spark a conversation. Even having gone to the same university can create an immediate bond with people. I wouldn't go as far as looking up their other social media profiles – unless they are the company's official ones, or Twitter - as it can, instead, feel intrusive when you start discussing their children and pets.

Starting a relationship from common ground helps break the ice twice as fast and can build a relationship of trust at a very profound, human level.

Beyond that, mind your body language.

First, wear your most authentic smile. Even if you're not a 'smiler', do it; try it in the mirror that morning whilst getting ready. Smile genuinely, like they're someone you've longed to meet since you were 10. That means smiling with both your mouth and your eyes. People can detect a fake smile from miles away, especially when just the corners of your mouth lift and the smile doesn't reach the eyes.

If you really struggle to project authenticity, author Olivia Fox Cabane[29] suggests that visualising a smile can improve your real smile. Think about a happy memory, a person close to your heart, and then imagine meeting that memory or person. Automatically, your smile will become genuine.

---

29 O. Fox Cabane, *The Charisma Myth: How Anyone Can Master the Art and Science of Personal Magnetism*. Portfolio Penguin, 2013

Second, shake their hand like Dwayne "The Rock" Johnson would. Firm, strong, confident - even if you're a petite woman. Personally, I can't think of anything more off-putting than a weak handshake, where it feels like you are shaking a lifeless piece of chicken. It implies that the person you're shaking hands with can't be bothered to do it, and as a result, they can't be bothered to be there with you.

In contrast, a firm handshake has the advantage of communicating to the other person your full presence in the moment, but also your strength. That makes a world of difference when establishing your position in the future relationship with your client.

Fox Cabane suggests the following steps for the 'gold-star handshake':

1. Keep your right hand free.

2. Use plenty of eye contact, and smile warmly but briefly.

3. Keep your head straight and face the other person.

4. Keep your hand perpendicular, thumb pointing straight to the ceiling.

5. Get full palm contact by draping your hand diagonally downward.

6. Wrap your fingers around your counterpart's hand.

7. Once you make full contact, squeeze to their level of firmness.

8. Shake from the elbow, step back, and then let go.

4. Understand Your Client's Personality

You've started building rapport. Now, it's very useful to begin understanding your client's personality.

To accomplish that, you needn't be a psychologist. A little bit of time spent considering the type of personality your client has will give you a greater chance of selling sustainability to them effectively. Why? Because business is always done from person to person. You don't actually buy things or products, or concepts; rather, you sell and buy to and from people.

So, your best chance to successfully conclude any business transaction – or to convince another person to buy into your ideas, whatever that is – is to "at-tune" with them. This means flexing your style to the *type* of person you have in front of you.

What's a very simple method for identifying your client's personality type? Mine is loosely based on studies from Carl Young and William Marston.

It can be summarised by the image below, made of four key character traits that we all broadly fall into.

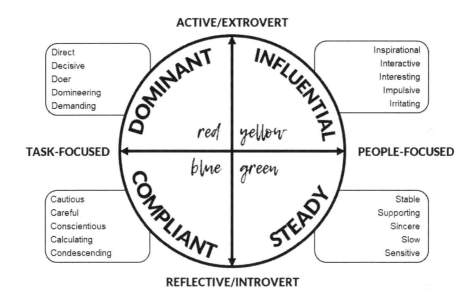

These are active vs. reflective (or extroverts vs. introverts, if you prefer) and task-focused vs. people-focused. The combination of these four character traits gives the four main DISC personalities (which are Dominant, Influential, Steady, and Compliant).

Let me give you some examples:

Damien is a Managing Director at Disc Manufacturing.

He has little time to waste; he's always on the go, so his meetings are gener-ally short and to-the-point. He talks with his hands, gets bored easily, and can be blunt. He wants his company to become the best in its sector, and he thrives on challenges.

Damien is very self-assured and knows what he wants. He's a man on a mission. He can be very demanding and domineering.

Which two personality characteristics does Damien have?

Damien is obviously active and task-focused. He falls into the "Red" quarter of the disc: the Dominant section.

Sara is Head of HR at Disc Manufacturing.

She is calm and patient, loves being helpful, and loves her job. She dislikes the spotlight, believes in the power of collaboration, and highly values loyalty and security. You might not get any clues from her facial expressions, and she speaks at a steady, easy pace. Her motto is "Slow and steady wins the race".

She can be indecisive, and might take disagreements personally.

Sara is people-focused and reflective, which makes her a "Green" or Steady person.

Imogen is Head of Marketing and Events at Disc Manufacturing.

She knows everyone in the sector. She is optimistic, enthusiastic, and thrives in gathering people around her. Imogen loves her social life. She uses many facial expressions and hand gestures when she talks. She can put you in touch with anyone you please, but you need to remind her, because she can easily forget. She's a bit loud and impulsive at times.

Imogen falls in the "Yellow" or Influential section, since she is people-focused and active.

Carl works in the engineering department of Disc Manufacturing.

Carl is brainy and a little geeky. He's in his element when he designs the technical details of products, and loves the logic of his job. He takes pride in the quality of his work, he can be very cautious, and he needs to ponder before making a decision. He dislikes socialising too much. You'll often see him with his arms folded and a hand on his chin.

Carl is reflective and task-focused, which makes him a Compliant - or "Blue" - personality type.

Think about someone you know; perhaps a current client or a colleague. What personality types do they incarnate?

It's also wise to reflect on your own profile and personality. At the moment, you might speak to people in a way that suits your own personality type. However, in order to sell effectively to anyone, you need to flex your style to suit other personality types.

Let me clarify: you don't need to change as a person. You will still need your authenticity when dealing with clients, but you can learn to flex your style and present facts in a different light or format. When speaking to them, you can choose words a little more carefully, according to the personality you're dealing with.

Naturally, the world is not split exactly into four. You'll find that some people are a crossover of the profiles, having a dominant colour and secondary colour traits, too. Additionally, we all evolve and change in time, so the colours of our personalities will also shift.

The key is to quickly identify which dominant trait your client has, and then focus on understanding their personality in the initial conversations you share with them. You can learn a great deal about people and their personality from how they write emails, speak during phone conversations, or use their body language.

That's an enormous help when determining the style you have to adopt, so you can move them towards your goals. When you understand the person in front of you, and adapt your style to connect with them at the same level, you're selling effectively.

Many CEOs and directors will fit inside the red section − extroverts, vision-driven, focused on a plan.

Scientists, engineers, and technical people generally fit inside the blue section − introverts, analytical, driven by objectivity.

If your client is a Red or Dominant, you may want to speak to them face-to-face or via phone, instead of sending lengthy emails.

Solicit immediate reactions and be prepared for them to take, or expect, immediate action. Reds may be more receptive to sustainability's return-on-investment benefits, and how certain decisions will affect their bottom line.

What if they are Green, or Steady?

Show sincere interest in them. Don't force them to take action; allow them to think about the subject and reach their own conclusions. Acknowledge their values and focus on the positive benefits that sustainability has on people and communities, as well as the long-term and security benefits for their company.

With Yellows, or Influential people, describe the overview before the details, discuss the meaning of the information or data, emphasise the big picture, and identify opportunities and challenges. Use your best inspirational storytelling to move them towards your sustainability goals. Show them how sustainability can make them and their company the most popular; perhaps suggest running for awards!

With Blues, or Compliant people, focus on concrete facts, discuss the steps involved in the correct sequence, have a clear purpose for the meeting, create an agenda that you've both agreed on, and stick to the timescale given. Be ready with all your detailed facts and figures, so you can back up your claims. With Blues, the risk management advantages of sustainability can be a winning argument, since it appeals to their cautious nature. Also, if you can demonstrate that your solution is the most logical, from a technical point of view, you're on the winning side.

The table below summarises the approach you can take, as well as the sustainability benefits to leverage when dealing with different personality types.

THEIR PERSONALITY	YOUR COMMUNICATION STYLE	WINNING SUSTAINABILITY BENEFITS	DO	AVOID
RED / Dominant	Direct, decisive, doer, domineering	Fast and energetic, big picture approach, face-to-face, to-the-point	Return on investment, cost savings, competitive advantage, productivity	Provide solutions not opinions, solicit (and expect) immediate action, show tangible benefits, use logic	Small talk, lengthy emails, fluffy arguments
YELLOW / Influential	Inspirational, interactive, impulsive	Personal, positive and imaginative approach, open and enthusiastic	New opportunities, inspirational views, market differentiation, brand awareness, attracting talent, Innovation	Summarise the key points and ask them to commit to a plan, show how (high profile) others have done it successfully, allow them to think aloud and change their mind	Too much detail, formal or rigid approach
GREEN / Steady	Stable, supportive, sincere, slow	Steady and personal talk, focus on values and areas of agreement	Positive impact on people and the planet, long-term security / resilience, attracting talent, risk management	Show sincere interest, build the relationship, deliver on promises, send info in advance, allow for reflection time, minimise risks	Fast action, pushing for an immediate response, burdening them with impersonal data
BLUE / Compliant	Cautious, careful, conscientious, calculating	Business-like, logical and structured	Technical advantages, risk management, long-term security / resilience, due diligence	Prepare in advance, provide plenty of details and logical arguments, be direct, allow for reflection time	Imprecision and fluffy arguments, excessive extroversion, pushing for an immediate response

The more you practice this technique, the faster you can understand the type of person in front of you and flex your style accordingly.

And the more you attune yourself with another person, the better you'll move them towards your goals.

5. Ask the Right Questions

At the kick-off meeting with any new client, you should focus on exploring their business, aspirations, challenges, plans, budget, needs, and wants as much as possible.

Remember, *needs* and *wants* can be very different things.

Sometimes, by asking the right questions, you will uncover issues or opportunities that not even your audience knew existed.

Let me give you an example.

Imagine you're at the seaside. Whilst you are strolling down the waterfront, you pass by a fish and chips shop (apologies for the very stereotypically British scenario), and your three year-old child asks you for a big bag of chips. Being health-conscious and a parent, you say no. Of course you do.

And you start:

"No, because you're going to spoil your appetite for the delicious kale and hummus sandwich I made for you" (or whatever stupendously healthy lunch you packed).

"No, because that would give you tummy ache."

But your child insists. Now, have you asked her *why* she wants those chips so badly?

If you did, she might've told you that she wanted to feed the birdies. She'd seen seagulls eating leftover chips earlier.

So it's bird seed you need to buy her. You could have explained that to her and saved yourself 10 minutes of drama.

Sakichi Toyoda, a father of the Japanese industrial revolution, developed the "Five *Whys*" technique in the 1930s. He was an industrialist, inventor and founder of Toyota Industries. His method became popular in the 1970s, and Toyota still leverages it to solve problems today.

It entails investigating the root of a problem by asking the people experiencing it *"why"* five times, until you reach the actual issue. Often, we jump into solution mode instead of seeking out the actual root of a problem. It's like alleviating pain from a broken bone with paracetamol, rather than fixing the bone itself.

For practicality, asking *"why"* three times (instead of five) is usually just as effective. Have you asked your clients *why* they want or don't want sustainability in their project? And, in detail, *why* they want certain features?

When I worked at BRE, a client for one of our training products was a university. I went to meet them, and they showed me around. One of the buildings was BREEAM Excellent certified. Fantastic! It looked the part. However, they showed me that, behind a metal fence, there was a huge, bright-red biomass boiler - like an eye-sore in the middle of the campus. Brand-new and never used, not even once.

They told me, with evident disappointment, that this portion of the sustainability kit cost them tens of thousands of pounds, but was left to rot. They were using the secondary gas boiler system, which, although inefficient, was much easier to use and responded better to their needs. I was astonished. Their BREEAM assessor obviously did a good job of helping them obtain an Excellent rating *on paper* - but that was their only objective, not the *actual* sustainability of the building and, core to this, the needs of their client.

I bet that assessor didn't ask *"why"* three times.

Then, of course, the client blamed the BREEAM system for being absurd and expensive. They needed a great building to teach students in, which operated sustainably and demonstrated to the students that the university walked the talk. The assessor heard: BREEAM Excellent, with whatever random system can get them there.

What a spectacular lack of communication and listening skills!

Do They Know What Sustainability Really is?

Let me give you another example.

A prospect comes to you, explaining that they need to build a shopping centre. They want it to be the flagship of their chain, but they cannot apply sustainability principles, because the shopping centre is close to an airport.

When you start to investigate their reasoning, they explain that the local authority has expressed concerns over the use of solar panels near the airport. There are potential risks of glint and glare, and potential interference with aeroplanes' navigation equipment.

As seen earlier, PV panels and wind turbines often equate sustainability in a client's mind – and some professionals' too.

They don't see how sustainability is a way of building and managing projects. It strives to have as little impact on the environment (and the people) as possible, and even enhances the environment the project sits in.

So you have a choice: you can tell your client that you'll research the subject and come back to them on the solar issue - there are many studies about how solar panels pose very few risks regarding glint, glare, and interference with airport equipment. Or, perhaps better, you can tell your client that sustainability is made of many wonderful things, and you can have a perfectly sustainable building without solar panels, while still achieving a flagship sustainable development.

Dr. Peter Bonfield, CEO of BRE at the time, once showed me an aerial photo of the London Olympic Park under construction. He worked with the Olympic Delivery Authority to help create and deliver the Sustainability Strategy, and led the procurement of construction products for the London 2012 Olympic Games.

He asked, "What can you notice, Virginia?"

He had the power to make you extremely uncomfortable, and put you on the spot with sometimes cryptic questions…

I started mumbling. "Ehm ehm… Cranes? Concrete buildings? A tidy construction site?"

He hastily said, "Yes, yes, but what else?"

Panic.

What could I see there, that was so remarkable?

He finally put me out of my misery and slyly said, *"No solar panels."*

The London Games were the greenest games in history, and carbon foot-printing informed decisions at the summer Olympics for the first time, in features like venue design, equipment selection, and game-time operations. The equivalent of 400,000 tonnes of carbon dioxide were saved in contrast to the original estimates. The Games' operations carbon footprint was 28% lower than planned. There was a 34% reduction in venue energy use, saving the equivalent of 31,000 tonnes of carbon dioxide.[30]

Without solar panels.

Sustainability is mainly composed of invisible things. In fact, it's the opposite of showing off fancy bits of equipment. Yet, not many people know that.

> *"People don't buy what you do, they buy why you do it."*
> Simon Sinek, author

Let's go back to your clients' "why".

Author Simon Sinek explains how everything begins with the "why". The purpose of any action you take is how it connects you with your audience. If you can align emotionally with your clients, your connection is much stronger and more meaningful than any affiliation based on features and benefits.

The purpose of your actions must be crystal clear in your head if you want to influence others, but, more importantly, you need to acknowledge the "why" of your client. Why should they adopt the solutions you're proposing? What's in it for them?

1. Start by connecting to your client's purpose.

2. Then, explain how you are going to deliver that vision.

---

30 www.olympic.org/news/london-2012-s-sustainability-legacy-lives-on

3. And, finally, you can talk about the features of the solutions.

You can tell from my "solar panels near the airport" story that asking *why* your client does or doesn't want something - and asking multiple times - will strip down any misunderstandings or misconceptions. It will unveil the heart of the client's objectives. That's why it's so important to just listen.

In new jobs, that first hour of the first meeting is perhaps the most important. Here is where you define the brief, but also where you have an opportunity to influence your client more than ever. Why? Because the key figures who make decisions and pay for the project may also be in the room - so take advantage of it.

If your client asked you to present what your business or expertise can offer them, great. Do that in five minutes. You don't need longer than that to present your credentials in a concise, to-the-point way. Don't brag about your qualifications, or the fact that your firm has been around for 50 years. Instead, showcase previous experiences in a couple of slides, so long as they're relevant to this project (for example, you've worked on a similar project, you had similar constraints, you know the local authority and regulations well, etc.). This will prove what you can do for your client, instead of uselessly showing off how great you are.

Then, spend the other 55 minutes asking your client or prospect questions - especially if they're in charge and make the decisions. Ask open questions about their vision for the project, and what expectations they have for sustainability. Try and gauge if these expectations can be fulfilled in the time, location, and budget you have available.

Those are the all-important '*why*'s for this project, which outline the aspirational goal.

With that said, here's a little word of advice: when you're meeting a client for the first time, if you believe they're one of these cynical naysayers, don't use the 'S' word. Just avoid using the term 'sustainability' as much as you can.

My dad proudly declares that he doesn't like any food that isn't Italian. He's proud of his heritage, and thinks Italian food is the only kind that agrees with his body and doesn't give him a stomach ache. When I'm cooking something vaguely exotic – like curry – I've learnt to simply place it before him and make him try it. To his credit, he gives me the benefit of the doubt and tries it. But I'm careful not to name the dish, instead offering it based on its qualities: *"You like rice and spicy food, dad, don't you? Try this."*

Often, if I name the dish, he samples it with a strange grimace and then doesn't like it. If I leave it nameless for the taste-test, there's a chance he'll enjoy it and even ask for the recipe.

I believe that sustainability is a synonym for quality, future-proofing, common sense, and responsibility. No-one wants to be accused of running an 'irresponsible' business, and everyone wants their venture to survive and thrive in the future, so alternative definitions may work just as well. As such, use the synonyms that can resonate with your client, and don't name the 'sustainability' dish at all.

People are biased towards labels. They either love them or hate them, so remove the label and just present the content. Chances are, they will like the dish.

Execute the Why, How, What

In practice, talk about:

- The "why" (the end result for your client).

- Then talk about "how" you are planning to implement it.

- And, finally, discuss the "what" (name its ingredients, talk about its features).

Why

The most important question of all remains the same: *"Why?"*

- Why do they want a flagship project (or why not)?

- Why are they discarding sustainability so quickly? What do they think it means?

If you can explain to them the basic principles, that's a golden opportunity. Someone that has no knowledge on the subject will be much easier to work with because:

- They will trust you; you are the expert after all.

- They won't need to unlearn any incorrect knowledge they have, which takes effort and commitment.

Therefore, if time allows, dispel any myths regarding sustainability – or at least try and understand if they have misconceptions, and start addressing them.

The main principle is KISS (Keep It Super Simple). In the next chapter, you'll find more techniques for communicating the core messages to your clients in simple (yet not trivial) ways.

How

The "how" element is quite important, especially when the client hasn't commissioned a similar project before. When gaining trust from your client, it's fundamental to explain the step-by-step process and clearly highlight how the various milestones will be reached. Why?

1. It proves you know what you're talking about.

2. It makes a project easy to understand and proceed with.

3. As such, it helps avoid potential issues caused by a lack of understanding from your client.

As a bonus, it's an opportunity to influence and inspire them to jump on board and support you in the process.

Just remember to use simple, everyday language. If you must use technical terms, be ready to explain them.

What

The final element - the 'what' - can be discussed with those who will practically implement your ideas from the client's side. Unless senior executives have a personal interest in engineering the idea, this final element will be discussed in depth with less senior, operational people in the company.

In the case of a sustainability project, they can be the IT guys, the designers, the engineers, the manufacturing department, and so on.

6. Get to Know the Project and Context

Aside from getting to know your client and what *they claim* their issues are, I strongly recommend this strategy:

Ask them to send through any relevant documentation, disclose any pre-existing decisions - send anything that can help you get under the skin of it all. Then, take the time to comb through it with an unbiased eye. As an expert, you might spot not only the risks, but also the opportunities that your client has missed. Thoroughly evaluating the project *and* your client will open up a world of possibilities, as well as avoid potential issues.

Equally important, you must understand the *context* around your project. When looking for clues, remember to check for PESTLE:

Political – What current government incentives and drivers are there to implement sustainability? Is the local authority imposing or encouraging sustainable commerce, or punishing those who don't comply with certain regulations?

Economic – How is the project funded? Is access to Green Finance a possibility here? Are there any public-funded capital programmes, or energy efficiency and low- and zero-carbon technologies incentives that you can tap into?

Social – How will the project impact the community it sits in? How is the community responding to new projects in the area? Can the community be welcomed to comment on the project and support its development? Buy-in from a community is often very powerful in the eye of the local authority. It's a marketing move and, of course, a good thing in its own right.

I'd also suggest looking into how the project's development will be handled, and by whom. This is often a major risk in any project. Does the team look well-assembled and competent to you? Are all responsibilities clearly defined? (I'll talk more about people in the chapter on People and Project Management)

Technological – What technological challenges does the project present? Modern methods of construction? Alternative production methods? Traditional natural materials? Building Information Modelling? Robotics? Circular economy?

Legal – Are there any health and safety considerations to be aware of? Local and national regulations that rule the project?

Environmental / Ethical – What is the location like? Are there any constraints linked to the project because of its geographical context? Any natural hazards? Any ethical labour concerns?

Also, what are the big wins you can bag from an environmental perspective through this project? What's a no-brainer that can be the focus of your pitch to the client?

A SWOT (strengths, weaknesses, opportunities, threats) analysis can also help you evaluate the project as a whole, finding issues and opportunities before digging into the details.

The goal of this prep-time and PESTLE analysis is to generate a tailored solution to your client's needs, rather than jumping into solution mode at the first meeting.

So long as your client's deadlines will allow it, analyse the project thoroughly before providing a comprehensive solution. Your client will appreciate that you've taken time to deliver a bespoke package, instead of a box-standard one.

7. Sell to Their Pain Point

At this stage, once you've made their primary objective crystal-clear, you must sell to their *pain point*: the issues that keep them up at night.

Find out what worries them, and match that with the perfect sustainability solution. I can't tell you what that is, because this is a very tailored approach.

However, your preliminary research and technical knowledge is fundamental in unlocking these doors of the project.

If your client objects that sustainability is difficult, fluffy, or not important; that they don't have the budget or resources for it; that the world is doomed anyway; that their project is too small to adopt sustainability principles; and so on… You needn't be defensive. Instead, ask again *why* they think that is.

Then you'll have the perfect opportunity to understand their fears and concerns, and respond precisely by dispelling the myths. Remember, it's not a debate. You want to serve your client, so help them achieve their objectives by using sustainability as a *tool*. You're on the same team, even if it doesn't always appear so. Sometimes, your client may need a little help or a bit more information on the subject, since their heart is in the right place.

Your ability to influence your client will determine the success of any sustainability project. The power is in your hands. (I'll talk about how you can influence your clients in the next chapter.)

8. Put Everything in Writing

This may seem like a lack of trust on your part, but it's crucial to any decision you manage to secure - especially from top management, whom you may have the good fortune of only meeting once. Make sure the decisions are written down accurately; and not on the back of an envelope, but in a sustainability brief, signed off by the client.

Your takeaways from that all-important first meeting should be:

- A *formal commitment* from the client to undertake a sustainability project with clear targets (it's difficult to have meaningful results if specific targets aren't chosen and agreed upon).

  If your project is an asset, like a building, it's worth mentioning here that sustainability is a life-long commitment for a building owner (if they'll also be responsible for the building's operations). A great, sustainable design will be meaningless and fail to work as intended if there is no commitment to operating the building as it was designed to be, if the facility manager is not on board, or if the building users are unaware of the sustainability features or how that building should be operated.

♦ Sustainability objectives must be put together in a *sustainability brief* and embedded in every contract and tender, especially those with the supply chain.

In construction, 80% of construction budgets are typically delivered by subcontractors. As such, they will be, by and large, responsible for the successful delivery of sustainability in every project. Choosing the right contractors (with sustainability experience and credentials) is fundamental to developing a sustainable building. The same goes for manufacturing of any goods, from fashion to food.

Now that supply chains extend around the world, sustainability (and the lack thereof) is an element that can affect any business quite significantly. Chains of custody, the way materials are extracted/harvested, and how products are manufactured must be verified before production starts. In particular, environmental and ethical objectives around modern slavery should be specified, especially in countries where laws in this respect are relaxed or nonexistent.

How to Be a Successful Sustainability Professional in a Country Where Sustainability is Not a Priority

Pantelis Levantis was a client of mine during my work at BRE. He's one of those resourceful construction professionals that, after having established themselves in their country in the traditional construction sector, now wanted to differentiate themselves. Pantelis lives in Greece and, as we know, Greece hasn't had the easiest ride in recent years, with a crippling recession that's created many casualties in the job market.

So, how exactly did Pantelis manage to not just survive, but also to thrive in Greece as a sustainability professional?

If you're in a country that's less familiar with sustainability, or deeply stuck in a traditional way of thinking, read on; you might find this example inspiring.

Pantelis founded Ecoveritas in 2011. Ever since, he has been the leader of sustainability in Greece, right in the middle of the economic crisis. During his interview for Green Gorilla Conversations, he described an interesting phenomenon:

He and his team found that, during the severe crisis, people were generally more open-minded to new perspectives - anything that would get them out of a pickle. But, fundamentally, it was easier to target international companies that had headquarters in Athens. Obviously, these companies were affiliated with other countries, which hosted more mature sustainability environments; it was easier for them to listen and understand what Pantelis had to say.

So, Ecoveritas managed to land several BREEAM certification advisory jobs, and gain a lead in the market. However, technical expertise by itself didn't convince their prospective clients to go with Ecoveritas' proposition. Pantelis explained that he strongly believes technical knowledge was only a prerequisite, and decisions are sometimes about politics, sometimes about marketing. As such, the main factor is to evaluate the people in front of him - understand their background, what they do understand, what they perceive - and then speak to them accordingly.

This factor played into every successful sale he made.

Pantelis gave me an example: you attend a meeting to win a client, where you're faced with an engineer, a CEO (Chief Executive Officer), and a CFO (Chief Financial Officer). As we've learnt, you have to speak about different concepts using different terminology that's tailored to each of them.

For example, when addressing the CFO, you can discuss minimising risk. That rings bells for them. When you talk with the CEO, you should use words such as "leadership" and "innovation." When you're speaking with the engineer, you have an easier task: you discuss saving energy, water conservation, and all the technical stuff.

Because the decision-maker is usually not the technical guy, it's wise to try and go up the chain and meet with the senior executives if possible. If you finish with the decision-makers, you have a better chance of closing the deal quickly and efficiently.

Now, you've completed your research on the person you're meeting, you've evaluated their company's attitude towards sustainability, and you've investigated the project. Ready for the hard-hitting stuff? Let's explore how to sell to your client or prospect.

Key Points to Remember

Feel free to use this space for jotting down notes on your personal takeaways from this section.

The "HOW": How to Deliver the Message Powerfully

Imagine that your client wants to produce sustainable T-shirts. They're asking for your advice.

Your client may have an idea of what "sustainable" means; for example, they think of buying organic cotton, because pesticides and insecticides haven't been used in the production.

However, you, as a sustainability professional, will have a wider perspective. You understand that there are other, more sustainable textiles than cotton - like bamboo, which uses around 1/3 of the water needed for growing cotton; is naturally antibacterial, so doesn't require pesticides; and grows quickly.

Furthermore, you know the most sustainable method is to avoid using new materials altogether. So, what about using recycled textiles? What are the energy implications of that when compared to sustainable new materials? What about a quality clothing-swap business instead?

Because you're an expert, you're aware of a wider set of elements. However, whilst there are some absolute answers (for example, the most sustainable material for a certain project), some of them might not be feasible for your client or in line with their ethos.

You're providing them with a service. You are a curator that sifts through the information available and seeks out the right match for their client.

It's equally crucial to develop a roadmap for your client to work from. By clarifying the important milestones and how to achieve them you will make their life much easier. This will entail who will need to be involved in the process, by what time, and what it's likely to cost. (More on this in the People and Project Management chapter.)

So, part of selling sustainability is showing your client how you plan to help them reach their goals.

The final 'how' is the way you communicate that message to them. I'll assume you have the key technical facts.

In my early BRE days, we used to support clients that had complex projects (which wouldn't fall within the standard BREEAM frameworks) by creating a bespoke framework. We visited clients to understand their projects and the key elements that had to be included in the BREEAM assessments.

At the beginning, I shadowed my senior colleagues in these kick-off meetings. As I described in the Note to the Reader of this book, I still remember how, after a brief look at the building plans, my colleagues would open the BREEAM manual and read from it, word by word. If you don't know, that's a 400-page volume, full of technical compliance criteria for evaluating sustainability in buildings. Those that had worked in the industry for a while would quote it by heart in a monotone voice to the baffled clients - acronyms, technical terms, and all.

Where was the rapport building? Where was asking the clients what they really wanted – or needed? Where was the understanding of their personalities, or their company's drivers and goals?

So, how can you *sell* sustainability to your client instead?

Let's assume you have prospective clients that are interested in buying your services. You just have to convince them to adopt a sustainability strategy.

Assuming you've done your homework (and, as such, are familiar with both the company and the individual you're speaking to), now it's all down to personal rapport; your ability to empathise with your clients and negotiate.

People buy from people, not from companies.

Have you ever watched Dragons Den (or Shark Tank, or any other title this popular programme has in your country)? In the programme, some tycoons receive pitches from hopeful inventors and entrepreneurs in search of investment and mentorship. Often, the 'dragons' don't invest in the *idea*, but in the *entrepreneur* - and they're vocal about it. When they can or can't work with the entrepreneurs, they're clear that it's not because of the product or idea, but because of the inventor and their personality.

Remember, people buy from people, not from companies.

Entrepreneurs who have walked out of the Dragons' Den with an investment are those with a vision, a good sense for numbers, and a good idea, of course.

But, they are also those who are likeable, personable, easy to work with, and professional.

This is what you should aspire to.

The Best Influencing Techniques to Sell Sustainability

The ability to 'sell' a concept that isn't tangible - like a sustainability strategy - takes more effort than, say, selling a shower head that eliminates limescale and saves water.

If you were selling the shower head, you could demonstrate how the water comes out softer than a standard shower head, or how increased pressure decreases the amount of water used. You can demonstrate it, and the prospective client can see or feel it on their skin. You could boil water from a standard shower head and show them the limescale accumulation, versus the softer water. These are all very practical tests that clearly show your client the product's benefits.

But how can you *show* your client the advantages of a sustainability strategy?

We've previously learnt that people broadly fall within certain psychological categories.

The best influencing technique will depend on the person in front of you and what makes them tick. That's why it's important to understand their '*why*', their personality, and do some research beforehand.

- ◆ Some have a **no-nonsense, scientific approach.** Think about Compliant-Blue types, but also Dominant-Red types. Be mindful that Reds may not want several details, but will prefer reaching a conclusion quickly and matter-of-factly. Providing compelling data in a logical manner, with good reasoning, can perform wonders on them. As such, be prepared to have all your research, percentages, and ROI calculations on hand for those stakeholders. Likewise, leverage some degree of storytelling to keep data alive and memorable; use your case studies, images, and graphs.

This combo will be your best chance of gaining your audience's attention in most cases.

- However, others, especially **the visionary** (Influential-Yellow types, for example, but also Steady-Green types, who are moved by feelings) **can be inspired.** Use storytelling techniques and show how others have done it before, or depict a future where your potential clients have achieved goals like no-one else has done before. This is a great way to influence people with a strategic mind and role.

- You can also make your potential clients **"feel good"**, by describing how their positive impact will be relevant in the grand scheme of things. This technique can be very powerful, especially when you align this vision with their CSR goals.

- **Reciprocity** can work when, for example, you're trying to influence a colleague or another peer. You do something for them, they do something for you.

- **Asking:** Depending on the situation, and the audience, you can ask for their opinion: *"What would you do in this case?"* Involving your client in the process will make them feel empowered.

- Show your audience that **they are not alone.** People are generally scared of change, so proving that others have done it before - and successfully - can help them feel like less of a maverick. This is a great technique for influencing risk-averse people, such Steady-Green people and Compliant-Blue people. With a slightly different accent, this is a powerful technique for Influential-Yellow people too, because they'll want to be connected to, be like, or be better than others.

- **Authority:** *You have to do it.* The local authority, the law, or the Clean Air Act imposes it. There is no way out and no arguments. Authority has its place, and it reinforces the drivers, but beware that forcefulness doesn't always come across well. According to many of my colleagues' stories, this is the most-used influencing technique out there among sustainability professionals, but it doesn't necessarily foster collaboration and good, long-term relationships.

- **Fear.** Explain to your audience the consequences of *not* doing what's advised; the penalties, the fines, the loss in revenue, the loss of market share. Fear can be powerful because it's an emotion; as we'll learn in the next chapter, emotions act as a stronger motivator than facts and data. Use this technique sparingly, however, or else you'll become a scaremonger. Again, that might not foster collaboration.

Along with body language and voice, delivering your message confidently implies that you can keep others' attention whilst you speak. Your best tool for this is storytelling.

Why You Should Learn to Tell Stories

"Make me care" - please, emotionally, intellectually, aesthetically, just make me care.
-Andrew Stanton, storywriter at Pixar[31]

I am fascinated by storytelling and its incredible ability to influence people by tapping into their emotions, even those who, at first, won't budge. Once I understood how it can help technical people (and, in particular, sustainability professionals), I knew storytelling had to feature in the Green Gorilla Master-class Programme.

Storytelling is about presenting facts as compelling tales and anecdotes.

It's the primordial way of passing information from one person to the next, and it's the most basic method for humans to communicate. Our brains are wired to tell and listen to stories. It's how we learn faster and better.

But why is that?

If you have children, you may have heard about oxytocin, a.k.a. the "happy hormone", which is released when you bond with your newborn baby. It's even

---

31 I invite you to watch a magnificent TED Talk by Andrew Stanton, storywriter at Pixar, called "The Clues to a Great Story". That TED talk is the best possible introduction to storytelling.

injected into expecting mothers to induce labour. Oxytocin is produced after any emotional interchange with people, such as with hugging and cuddling.

Whilst researching for the Green Gorilla's Tell Compelling Stories course, I came across another brilliant TED Talk, by Dr. Paul Zak, PhD, professor of economics, psychology, and management at Claremont Graduate University. Dr. Zak uncovered the science behind why storytelling is good for business.

His lab discovered that the neurochemical oxytocin is a *"it's safe to approach others"* signal in the brain. Oxytocin is produced when we're shown kindness or trust, and it motivates cooperation with others by enhancing the sense of empathy and our ability to experience others' emotions. Empathy is important for social creatures, because it allows us to predict how others will react to a situation.

Your body produces oxytocin even when you watch a feel-good movie, one that pushes all the right buttons in your brain. The fact is, the brain does not distinguish between reality and fiction, and that's why movies provide such powerful entertainment, because your brain literally experiences the emotions you see in the movie as if they were yours. It activates the same areas as if you were undertaking the adventures you see on the screen, including jumping from a skyscraper, shooting, kissing, and so on.

The science behind oxytocin is incredibly relevant to you, even if you're a technical person reading this.

But why is that important to anyone who needs to influence others (let's face it, that's all of us)? Oxytocin has been demonstrated to increase the amount of *trustworthiness* in people listening to a story, or watching a movie.

When people become absorbed in a good story, their defences and judgements drop, their empathy and willingness to help increases, and they tend to trust the storyteller more than they would otherwise.

In subsequent studies[32] Dr. Zak's lab deepened their understanding of why stories motivate voluntary cooperation. He discovered that, in order to create a desire to help others, a story must first sustain attention – a scarce resource in the brain – by developing *tension* during the narrative. If the story creates that

---

32 www.hbr.org/2014/10/why-your-brain-loves-good-storytelling

tension, then attentive viewers/listeners will likely come to share the emotions of the characters. After it ends, they'll likely continue mimicking the feelings and behaviours of those characters.

He demonstrated that character-driven stories with emotional content result in a better understanding of the key points the storyteller makes. The audience can also better recall these points weeks later. As for making an impact, this blows the standard PowerPoint presentation to bits. People may hear data, but they feel stories. We remember our feelings way better than percentages.

As a technical person, you may like your data and facts.

However, facts and data, especially to someone like your client, who is likely not technical, have zero *impact if they're not contextualised and brought closer to human nature.*

Have you ever listened to a presentation that sent you straight to sleep? It was delivered in a monotone voice and consisted of a vast list of data and bullet points, read straight from the PowerPoint screen, provided without any injected life.

That's why people like case studies: because they translate data into digestible stories; they demonstrate how it's directly relevant to people's lives and businesses; and they have the double-whammy power of showing how others have done it before, validating your data further.

In a business context, you rarely have time to explore a whole story; you may have only 90 seconds to present your facts. But I encourage you to rethink how you deliver those 90 seconds.

Storytelling is a key skill that will bring your data to life. The human brain looks for stories everywhere, and it's fascinated by them. Remember when you were a child and looked at the clouds: you found characters, animals, even whole adventures playing in the sky. We look for recognisable patterns everywhere we go. So, learning how stories work (their structure, characters, and the all-important oxytocin and emotion triggers) may be the right ingredient to help you succeed.

Through stories and anecdotes, you'll manage to increase your clients' trust in you and prep them to listen to your arguments. Increasing their 'feel-good' hormones will connect them to you at a deeper level and create stronger human relationships. You don't even need to hug them! What's not to like?

The question now is: how can you do that?

First of all, we should define what makes a good story in the context of business or science.

Randy Olson, a marine biologist-turned-filmmaker, explores in his book *Houston, We Have a Narrative*[33] (forgive him, please, for the corny title) how the basic principles of storytelling can be applied to scientific work, which is typically made of dry data. He adopted a basic method that Trey Parker, co-writer of South Park, used when he got stuck in the famous cartoon's story.

He called it the ABT method: *And – But - Therefore.*

With this simple approach, when Trey Park couldn't advance past a dull part of the story, he would add a "BUT" - i.e. a twist; something that changed the narrative in an unexpected way, which then led to an enticing consequence that would spark interest in the viewers. Olson is very familiar with the world of science, and from his more recent work with Hollywood, he understands that much can be done to improve how scientific work is disseminated, without trivialising it.

Scientists live in a world of *And-And-And.* They list impersonal facts and, as a result, they don't get traction with their brilliant work. In other cases, you may find people using an overly narrative style or DHY (*Despite - However - Yet),* another type of pointless narrative that goes on (and on, and on) and never reaches the point.

In any good story, the tension created by a number of BUTs can dramatically influence how narrators successfully disseminate the content of their work.

These three structures are illustrated in the picture below.

33   R. Olson, *Houston, We Have a Narrative: Why Science Needs Story,* The University of Chicago Press, 2015

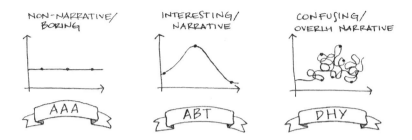

In our Storytelling Masterclass, we use a dice game, which is an idea I borrowed from Randy Olson. One dice has AAA, ABT, and DHY printed on its faces; one dice has generic conversation subjects, like sports, your weekend, pets, food, etc.; and one dice has specific sustainability subjects, like climate change, circular economy, net-zero energy, etc.

The game exercises your most basic storytelling muscles by rolling the AAA / ABT / DHY dice and the general conversation dice. Then, you tell a short story using the structure you rolled.

Depending on the structure used, it's immediately obvious whether the story gets more interesting, or more boring, or confusing. Once participants adjust to the basic structure for generic conversational topics, I challenge them to roll the sustainability dice. Then, they discuss a more technical subject using the different story structures - and, in particular, ABT - so they learn to add interest to their once boring or confusing stories.

Play the game with your colleagues using the virtual dice on the Green Gorilla website.[34] See whether you can begin telling more interesting stories.

ABT is the most basic story structure, but it provides a great starting point for anyone who tries storytelling for the first time.

Now, let's add some complexity.

Let me tell you a story (wink, wink!):

> *Sometimes the biggest obstacles turn out to be your biggest assets.*

> *It's 1974.*

---

34   www.thegreengorilla.co.uk/resources/abt-game

Steven Spielberg is a 27-year old movie producer, terrified of having his project Jaws yanked. At the time, he didn't have much experience as a director, aside from Columbo and a flop movie, The Sugarland Express.

The $250,000 mechanical shark, named Bruce after Spielberg's lawyer, is a disaster.

It sinks on its first day. It needs to be rescued, cleaned, and repainted every day of filming and it doesn't look realistic, with its pearl-white teeth and crossed eyes.

"I had no choice but to figure out how to tell the story without the shark...I asked myself, what would Hitchcock do in a situation like this?"

Spielberg comes up with the idea of an unseen enemy.

Jaws wins three Oscars and is the first film to top $100 million in the box office.

Can you see how, in the space of a few lines, you were already wondering: *"Jaws? The movie that still scares me over 40 years after its release, was a flop?"* Whilst reading, you quickly wondered how they managed to make such a compelling movie that triggers strong emotions (fear, in this case), with a crossed-eye mechanical shark. Tension was built in only four lines. And you can hear the theme of *Jaws* in your head, can't you?

If you dismantle this very brief story, it's clearly made of a few key elements.

I hate to tell you, but *every* story on this planet has, give or take, the same structure. Sorry for ruining all the movies you watch from now on…

The Hook

You have an initial statement, which is too vague to spoil the full story, but serves as a hook. You want to know how the biggest obstacles turn out to be your biggest assets.

This part is important, especially in a business context. Of course, you can begin with the story immediately, but a short introduction makes your audience decide whether or not to join you on this venture; whether or not to invest two minutes of their precious time in listening to you. That's their hook.

The Backstory

Then you have the backstory: when, where, who, and what happened prior to this moment.

The Tension

Next, you have the most important part. The clue lies in what Dr. Zak discovered with his scientific studies: tension (a.k.a. the "BUT" in Randy Olson's reflections). Tension, twists, and unexpected changes are what keep your audience engaged. These are triggers for your brain to feel emotion.

Think about the opposite: everything is well, nothing special is happening, it's all as it's always been (remember: and – and - and). Where is the interest there? Instead, something doesn't go to plan, the main character (or hero) has an itch they can't scratch.

In this case, the shark is not what Spielberg wanted; it's a total flop and the movie seems doomed. What does our hero long for? Why can't they obtain it? Drama and unexpected change is the heart of a good story. If there is no conflict, no drama, and no change, there is no story.

In movies, you typically experience several unexpected twists, which the writers sprinkle throughout to keep the tension high for the two hours you're sitting down, munching popcorn.

The Suspense

Now, there's another underlying lesson in the *Jaws* story: Spielberg discovered he could achieve an even better result for his movie by *not showing* the shark. The absence, in this case, is even more compelling and scary than seeing the character in the flesh. It's not always possible to construct a story this way, but if there's an opportunity to create *suspense*, then by all means - do it. This part needs to be orchestrated correctly. You should make the audience work for their meal. Don't tell them what's happening immediately; tease them. Humans are born problem-solvers. As such, in stories, the well-organised absence of information will draw your audience in. Give them 2 + 2, but don't give them 4.

The Breakthrough

Normally, at this point in a story, you reach the "eureka" moment. There's a breakthrough, either via a mentor, a situation, or an idea. Something or someone triggers it. That's the *a-ha* moment we were all waiting for.

The Journey

From here, there's a journey that the main character undergoes to pursue their new-found purpose. In our *Jaws* story, there isn't much of this, and the story works without knowing all the details - but we certainly can imagine them, because we know the movie.

The Victory/Lesson Learnt

Finally, there is the moment of victory: the Academy Awards for Spielberg, the resolution, and the happily ever after for everyone else. Often at this point you have your lesson learnt, or moral, of the story that connects back to the hook at the beginning, closing the circle.

Archetypes

When building your own stories, it's worth considering that all stories follow some 'archetypes'. These are certain patterns that repeat in human storytelling, which can be useful frameworks to help facilitate and guide the results (or emotions) you hope to obtain.

The more common are:

Coming of Age

After years of learning and growing, you've reached a milestone. You know who you are. You are strong, experienced, and confident. You're ready to take on whatever comes next.

- Use this archetype to show *experience* and *strength*.

Overcoming Obstacles

You hit a roadblock and almost failed. It was a struggle. You challenged your assumptions, made tough decisions, fought hard… and won.

-Use this archetype to demonstrate *resilience.*

Constant Evolution

You never rest. Over and over, you've evolved to handle whatever comes your way. You keep moving, adapt to the world around you, and maybe even anticipate its change.

- Use this archetype to prove *adaptability.*

True as It Ever Was

Your purpose and values have endured throughout the years.

The world has evolved and you've changed with it, but your core beliefs have remained intact. They guide everything you do.

- Use this archetype to communicate *steadiness* or to reinforce the audience's *trust.*

Rebirth

Over time, you've accumulated a wealth of experience and knowledge. Today, you're harnessing that to start a whole new chapter, and become an even better version of yourself.

- Use this archetype to explain a *new direction.*

Quest

You've always had a clear objective and you've pursued it relentlessly.

Over time, you've summoned your talent and passion to turn your vision into reality. Through twists and turns, you've maintained your focus, and you will never let it go.

- Use this archetype to *renew commitment* or *demonstrate dedication.*

Your Storytelling Language

Finally, let's evaluate the language you use to build stories, so that they make a lasting impression. Your message won't be persuasive if people can't understand it.

The Flesch-Kincaid Grade Readability Level, developed by the U.S. Navy to measure the difficulty of technical manuals used in training, is a great tool for checking if your audience is likely to understand your message.

This is based on a number of factors, including the length of sentences, the number of syllables used, and the types of words used (for instance, those that are unusual, jargon, etc.).

If a piece of text has a grade level readability score of 8, then the average reader needs a Grade 8 reading level (that's between 13 and 14 years old) or above to understand it.

There are readability tests available online, based on the Flesch-Kincaid method[35], which serve as easy resources for checking your stories or content. Paste your text into one of the many tools, click "go", and you'll receive your score.

Be sure to account for the kind of people in front of you: are they general public? Highly educated? Foreign? Technically trained? The lower the score on the Flesch-Kincaid scale, the lower the degree of knowledge and language skill your audience needs to understand your text.

As a rule of thumb, it's always best to use language that's simple to understand by most people. If your text has a higher score than your audience, use gentler synonyms for certain difficult words or rephrase the content, so your sentences are broken into more digestible, bite-size chunks.

---

35 Try https://app.readable.com/text/

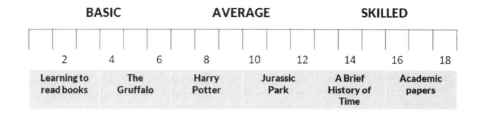

At this point, you may be wondering: *"How do I put all of this into practice?"*

Let me show you another example. Here, we have a sustainability story that doesn't have the right structure or language, and one that does.

> *There is significant evidence to suggest that buildings do not perform as well as* anticipated *at the design stage.*
>
> *Findings from the PROBE studies (Post Occupancy Review of Buildings and their Engineering) demonstrated that actual energy consumption in buildings will usually be twice as much as predicted.*
>
> *This was based on post-occupancy reviews of 23 buildings previously featured as 'exemplary designs' in the Building Services Journal (BSJ) between 1995 and 2002. More recent findings from the Carbon Trust's Low Carbon Buildings Ac-* celerator *and the Low Carbon Buildings Programme have demonstrated that in-use energy consumption can be five times higher than compliance calculations.*
>
> *Both studies suggest that lack of feedback following occupancy is one of the biggest contributors to this gap. Another key factor is that calculations for* regulatory com- *pliance do not account for all energy uses in buildings.*
>
> *These calculations are commonly* misinterpreted *as predictions of in-use energy consumption, when in fact they are simply mechanisms for compliance with Building Regulations.*
>
> Unregulated *sources of energy consumption such as small power loads, server rooms, external lighting, etc. are rarely considered at the design stage. Yet these typically account for more than 30% of the energy consumption in office buildings, for example.*

Let's analyse what's wrong with it:

- For a start, this text has a readability score of 13.8 in the Flesch-Kincaid scale. As such, only university-educated people can understand it; that's only 48% of the average general audience.

- There are several "hard" words, which are unusual and/or made of four syllables or more. I have highlighted them in the text.

- In this text, 60% of the sentences have more than 30 syllables - which means longer sentences that can tire or bore the reader. They make it hard to keep track of the meaning.

- It frequently uses a passive voice.

- The text is a sequence of *and – and – and.*

- The good news is, this particular story has a chance of becoming far more engaging, because it reveals facts that were unexpected.

What is a fast way of making any story instantly more engaging? Use a first-person perspective and personal anecdotes. I've created my version of the same story. The storytelling elements are clearly outlined and, here, I've used the "Overcoming Obstacles" archetype.

OLD STORY	NEW STORY	EXPLANATION
There is significant evidence to suggest that buildings do not perform as well as anticipated at the design stage.	The performance gap is a serious issue that the construction industry, as a whole, is trying to address.	*Hook* *I introduce the concept of performance gap in my version.*
	This is the difference between the way the buildings were designed to perform, and their actual performance once built. The performance gap is evident in many studies conducted in new, occupied buildings. Several factors can contribute to it: • Design errors • Design calculations in line with regulations, which do not account for up to 30% of energy uses in buildings (e.g. small power, external lighting, server rooms etc.) • Incorrect installation and commissioning of systems • Lack of feedback from the occupants to the designers after construction • Incorrect use of the buildings by occupants.	*I also explain it, so the story is more understandable.* *Here, I incorporate the key findings from the research.*
Findings from the PROBE studies (Post Occupancy Review of Buildings and their Engineering) demonstrated that actual energy consumption in buildings will usually be twice as much as predicted.		*I omit this fact, since the more impressive data is found in the following paragraphs.*
This was based on post-occupancy reviews of 23 buildings previously featured as 'exemplary designs' in the Building Services Journal (BSJ) between 1995 and 2002. More recent findings from the Carbon Trust's Low Carbon Buildings Accelerator and the Low Carbon Buildings Programme have demonstrated that in-use energy consumption can be 5 times higher than compliance calculations.	Recent studies from the Carbon Trust's Low Carbon Buildings Accelerator and the Low Carbon Buildings Programme focused on the performance gap. They found that buildings can consume up to a staggering five times more energy than predicted at the design stage. Just as I experienced first-hand.	*I highlight the key data here with a strong adjective.*

OLD STORY	NEW STORY	EXPLANATION
Both studies suggest that lack of feedback following occupancy is one of the biggest contributors to this gap. Another key factor is that calculations for regulatory compliance do not account for all energy uses in buildings.	In 2006, I was gathering data to finish my MSc dissertation on sustainability in healthcare buildings. I picked the Greenwich Millennium Health Centre as my case study. It was one of the most sustainable buildings back then. Built in 2001, it ticked all the right boxes: sustainable materials, high levels of air tightness and insulation, built on a brownfield site, and more.	*Backstory* *I make the facts more memorable by introducing a personal 'overcoming obstacles' story*
These calculations are commonly misinterpreted as predictions of in-use energy consumption, when in fact they are simply mechanisms for compliance with Building Regulations. Unregulated sources of energy consumption such as small power loads, server rooms, external lighting, etc. are rarely considered at the design stage. Yet these typically account for more than 30% of the energy consumption in office buildings, for example.	But then, the facility manager gave me its most recent consumption data. I started to analyse them. Surprisingly, the building was consuming twice as much electricity as intended, mainly in summer.	*Tension*
	At first, I couldn't understand why. The designers seemed to have designed the building correctly. The staff working within the centre had no clue where that extra consumption came from. I looked at all the possible reasons why this was happening.	*Tension*

OLD STORY	NEW STORY	EXPLANATION
	Only when I unpicked the issue with the facility manager did I realise where the problem laid. The building management system had been calibrated to provide shade to the south-facing windows. Every time the sun came out, the sun-shading awnings automatically opened. Then they automatically closed during windy spells – including at night. In the days when the weather was a mix of overcast and sun, the awnings would come in and out every few minutes. As a result, they consumed an enormous amount of electricity.	*Breakthrough*
	This was the first time I realised the importance of accurate building commissioning. It is key to marry design intentions with actual operation.	*Victory/Lesson Learnt*

Notice that I left percentages out of my story. It's definitely useful to cite a few data to validate your concept, especially in a business context (I mentioned the data I felt was most impressive), but littering your presentation with percentages is not useful. Of the average crowd, only 5% remember percentages, whilst 63% remember stories.[36]

If you *do* want to include data, select what is most relevant to your audience, then use charts and other visuals to bring it to life. If you're talking to decision-making clients, rather than engineers, it's even more vital to adjust your content and language for a non-technical audience.

In my iteration of the facts, I provided the hook and backstory, summarised the main concept, and then spent most of the time describing a real case that ensured the backstory and starting point were obvious and memorable to my audience. I also highlighted extremely relevant parts of the story with strong

---

36   C. Heath, D. Heath, *Made to Stick: Why Some Ideas Survive and Others Die*, Random House, 2007

adjectives and adverbs like "staggering" and "surprisingly", while using "but" to introduce a twist in the story.

To build up your storytelling muscle, start paying attention to the stories around you. Here there are some ideas:

- Read industry magazines.

- Pay attention to social media feeds from trustworthy sources - you don't want to spread fake news!

- Capture anecdotes in the wild that convey your message: listen to your colleagues chat whilst making tea; go to conferences; network; absorb what you see and hear.

- Mostly, though, think about your own stories. Remember experiences with past clients and projects, and consider how they demonstrate your point in a more digestible way. I'm sure you have plenty of interesting anecdotes from your own working life that you can polish and use in future presentations.

They don't have to be strictly related to work or to sustainability, either; they could be everyday life episodes that resonate in your professional life. Uncover the funny side to your work. A little joke, cracked at the right time, is a perfect way to break the ice in many situations.

Practise telling those stories, write them down if necessary, and tell them again and again, until they become second-nature.

To help you with this task, I have created a Green Gorilla Storytelling crib sheet, which you can download from the website to remember all the steps and elements covered in this chapter.[37]

When putting together your stories, don't be afraid to use pictures, charts, and other visuals as well. It will reinforce the concepts and increase memorability.

In fact, rethink your PowerPoint slides completely. Use big pictures, graphs, videos, and even cartoons to make them come alive. Challenge yourself to not

---

37   www.thegreengorilla.co.uk/sustainable-the-book

write anything on them besides a title, unless it's absolutely necessary – and never write more than five bullet points at the most, in a nice, big font size. This will prevent you from reading the slides and, instead, force you to learn the presentation by heart. As such, your delivery will be far less mechanical and far more authentic.

You can thank me later.

The "WHAT": Building the Business Case for Sustainability

Let's recap. It's time to put together everything we've discussed until this point. By now, you should know how to:

- Understand who's in front of you by using the DISC model.

- Understand their needs by asking "why" at least three times.

- Understand the project and its context by using the PESTLE model.

- Understand the company's current stage in their pursuit of sustainability.

- Convince them by using powerful influencing techniques, such as storytelling.

You also know your role in curating information for them and developing a plan of action.

Now, let's explore the content of your arguments: the *"what"*.

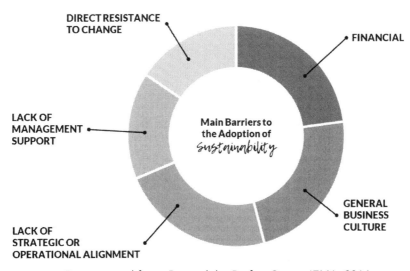

Data sourced from: Beyond the Perfect Storm, IEMA, 2016

When discussing the implementation of sustainability, it's no wonder that money is one of the primary barriers that organisations bring forward.

Money is the prime reason businesses exist. Anything that is *perceived* as out of line with the ethos of profit, sooner or later, gets dropped. That is, unless it provides some other, incontestable value that can't be easily dismissed,

As discussed earlier, sustainability gets a bad rep with regards to money. It's wrongly perceived as a fancy add-on; something easily stuck on the roof at the end, like a cherry atop a cake, which you can, of course, safely do without. Because of this, it's hard for sustainability professionals to shift the paradigm.

Sustainability is viewed as something that costs money, rather than makes money - that's the fundamental bottom line. It has yet to reach the point that health and safety obtained in recent years, where it's imposed by law and offers clear penalties that businesses everywhere view as too dire to ignore.

However, contrary to what the general public believes, sustainability is not a fancy add-on; it's not the cherry on top, but the cake itself! Indeed, sustainability is a synonym of quality.

The first step, then, is to try and focus on your clients' potential drivers.

If sustainability is not imposed by law, or local regulation, you'll need to find other drivers.

Now, I know plenty of consultants who, when there's even the smallest chance of sustainability being imposed from above, immediately use the stick. *"You must do it."* That's it. No arguments.

As explained in the chapter covering the Best Influencing Techniques to Sell Sustainability, this technique can work - with limitations. It prompts your client to sign on the dotted line, but that doesn't foster a particularly nice relationship. It's like an authoritarian parent; of course, they manage to keep a tight ship, but they don't earn respect from their children. You want the client to collaborate with you as much as possible; to feel like *they're* in charge, *they're* the hero of the story. That's how you create a happy client. Nobody wants to feel coerced, because as soon as there's an opportunity to escape and do what they want (i.e. ditch sustainability at the first hurdle, or reduce it to the bare minimum compliance), they will.

Instead, you can search out other drivers and incentives for your clients to embrace sustainability, and have a more active role in it – or even get excited by it!

The best sustainability professional will marry *benefits* with *client needs*, even the needs they're unaware of!

Start by pondering the needs of your specific client, using all the research you've performed until now to understand them, their business, the context, and the specific project. With it, you can suggest an exact solution for their unique problem.

For example, my client is a sportswear start-up trying to make their name in a crowded market. They want to explore ways of producing their garments sustainably.

What are their primary needs? They need to make money, of course. So sustainability will need to reduce costs for them.

I suggest carrying out an LCA of their garments, from the sourcing of materials to the disposal at the end of their life. With it, my client minimises costs by designing out waste, and reusing or up-cycling any byproducts. To cap it off, they'll cut overheads by operating exclusively online - which saves money, as well as energy to power any premises.

They also need to raise their profile and stand out in a saturated market. Millennials, their target market, prefer to spend their money on brands that demonstrate their commitment to the environment. By adopting an ethos based on the environment and ethics, my client can gain their target market's trust and set themselves apart from competition.

They can also set aside a budget to research new plant-based materials, which will swap out any plastic compound in their garments. After all, they need to reassure their customers they aren't just a fad; they walk the talk. There are already enough greenwashers out there!

Work your way through your clients' needs, and suggest sustainability benefits that fulfil each one of their needs.

Before you present this, however, you need to explain your intentions.

In our profession, we all know how sustainability is generally intended: as a way of thriving in the present without jeopardising the future by overusing our resources. This is true for each portion of a sustainable society: the famous 'Triple Bottom Line' of economy, people, and the planet.

To effectively sell sustainability to clients who are concerned about sustainability's expense on their business, we need to start by dispelling the myths: it's not all about becoming eco-druids, tree-huggers, and goody-goodies (although, from your point of view, the ethical aspect is probably a welcomed side effect). Rather, understanding and implementing sustainability is the best starting point towards earning more money and securing longevity in their business.

Let's start from the Triple Bottom Line. In this case, we will expand the definition by talking about another famous model of sustainable development: the Five Capitals model.[38]

- *Financial and Manufactured Capitals*

  First, sustainability strives to ensure that the capitals of finance (all the money-related assets we have as a society: banknotes, bonds, shares, etc.) and manufacturing (all the physical assets and goods that contribute to producing our 'stuff', like buildings, tools, machines, etc.) are healthy, without compromising the other capitals, or the future.

- *Society and Human Capitals*

  Then, there is the society capital (i.e. the institutions that help maintain our human capital, like families, communities, schools, volunteering organisations, etc.) and the human capital (that's the people's health, knowledge, skills, and motivation, which support human beings in doing their productive work).

- *Natural Capital*

  Finally, and most importantly, there is nature, which provides all the materials and energy needed to create everything. Ultimately, all things tie back to nature, so it's the most important capital of all.

---

38 www.forumforthefuture.org/the-five-capitals

Our clients need to understand that, for their businesses to thrive, all the capitals should increase. When done appropriately, they will thrive as a business and "live off the interest" - but that must be done sustainably (without negatively affecting the other capitals or jeopardising the future). As a bonus, this will make their businesses resilient in the face of global change's impact on any of the capitals.

But what arguments can you use to demonstrate this? How will you convince them that applying sustainability will provide an advantage when compared to business as usual?

Sustainability benefits can be summarised in three broad categories:

♦   Return on investment.

♦   Risk management.

♦   Growth.

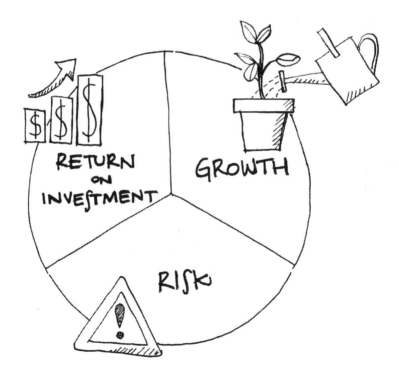

Let's explore the details of what each category includes.

Return on Investment

Bob Willard, a leading expert in the business case for sustainability, has demonstrated a startlingly positive fact via hundreds of case studies: on average, a small company of five employees and a $1 million turnover can increase its profit by 51% just by adopting standard sustainability practices (without being particularly innovative). A larger company of 1,000 employees and a $500 million turnover can increase its profit by 81%, when compared to equivalent companies that carry on as usual.

Increased Revenue and Market Share

Sustainability helps companies answer the market demand for sustainable products and businesses; it increases quality and allows companies to add a premium to their pricing structures.

- According to a 2018 global online consumer survey, conducted by Nielsen[39], 49% of global respondents were happy to pay a premium for items with high-quality/safety standards, which consumers often associate with strong sustainability practices. Consumers were also willing to pay more for items that are organic (41%), made with sustainable materials (38%), or deliver on socially responsible claims (30%).

- In 2019, NYU Stern's Center for Sustainable Business completed extensive research on U.S. consumers' actual purchasing of consumer packaged goods (CPG). They found that 50% of CPG growth from 2013 to 2018 came from sustainability-marketed products. They examined over 36 categories and more than 71,000 individual products, which accounted for 40% of CPG dollar sales over the five-year period. Products that had a sustainability claim on their packaging delivered nearly $114 billion in sales, up 29% from 2013. Most importantly, products marketed as sustainable grew 5.6 times faster than those that were not. In more than 90% of the CPG categories, sustainability-marketed products grew faster than their conventional counterparts.

---

39 www.nielsen.com/wp-content/uploads/sites/3/2019/04/global-sustaina-ble-shoppers-report-2018.pdf

- The added premium can also be viewed in the real estate sector, where it's now normal to charge more for rent and sales of sustainable buildings.

- Sustainability allows companies to explore new markets and opportunities, such as accessing green finance, green investments, and bids that require the demonstration of sustainable credentials. Let's not forget that, in some cases, companies must demonstrate their sustainability credentials to compete in public tenders – as is often true in U.K. construction.

  - In 2019, assets committed to divestment (shifting money out of the fossil fuel industry and into climate solutions that power the transition to a 100% renewable-energy future) leapt from $52 billion in 2014 to more than $11 trillion - a stunning increase of 22,000%. Institutions committed to divestment include sovereign wealth funds, banks, global asset managers and insurance companies, cities, pension funds, health care organizations, universities, and faith groups and foundations.

- A focus on sustainability means savings across the whole supply chain, including logistics, which can benefit a company's bottom line quite significantly. For example, Walmart, the U.S. discount retailer, aimed to double fleet efficiency between 2005 and 2015 through better routing, truck loading, driver training, and advanced technologies. By the end of 2014, they had improved fuel efficiency by approximately 87%, as compared to the 2005 baseline. In that year, these improvements resulted in 15,000 tonnes of CO_2 emissions avoided and savings of nearly $11 million.

Cost Savings via Reduced Energy Expenses

Energy and CO_2 are the two most used metrics of environmental sustainability - and rightly so. They've been demonstrated to have the biggest impact on global warming. Energy savings via energy efficiency practices have the double advantage of generating monetary savings for companies that switch to those practices, as well as reducing CO_2 pumped into the atmosphere. So, arguably, they should be everyone's priority.

Cost Savings via Reduced Waste Expenses

 ◆ It costs money to dispose of waste, both in landfill taxes and in fines whenever the rules are not followed. Designing out waste from companies' operations can help reduce costs both in production and disposal. As an example, in construction, the advent of Building Information Modelling has reduced miscalculation risks in quantity surveying, and both Modern Methods of Construction (MMCs) and off-site building offer lean construction techniques. As such, it's easy to see how the established practice of including a 10% extra contingency when procuring materials is starting to die off.

 ◆ With the Far East closing the doors to Western waste, transforming non-recyclable waste in heat and power is an efficient way to reduce energy costs and waste (otherwise destined to the landfill). Large Energy from Waste (EfW) plants like London's Cory Riverside collects and transforms around 750k tonnes of London's waste into energy and heat for the city, as well as building aggregates and blocks from the energy production residue.

Cost Savings via Reduced Materials and Water Expenses

 ◆ An acquaintance of mine worked as an engineer in the London's Crossrail project. He explained to me how eight million tonnes of excavated and construction waste material were generated during construction of the tunnels, shafts, station boxes, and caverns. An impressive 99.7% was beneficially reused. The surplus material was destined to form the Wallasea Island in Essex (a.k.a. Boris Island, named after the then Mayor of London, Boris Johnson). Nearly all of the Crossrail's excavated material was transported by train and ship along the River Thames, removing 150,000 lorries off the streets of London. The team saved millions by deploying certain materials as aggregates for the infrastructure itself. The rest was used to develop new wildlife reserves, recreational facilities, and agricultural and industrial land all along the Thames.

 ◆ The same goes for sustainability and water. Although water has been the cheapest of all commodities in the Western world for some time now, climate change - and the threat of longer hot spells, watercourse pollution, and draughts - means that water efficiency must now be seriously taken into consideration at the design table. In some parts of the world, water savings and efficiency are the norm, since potable water is scarce. A sustainable approach that favours reduction of water demand, promotion of water efficiency, and water reuse and recycling - in this order - will save money and secure self-sufficiency.

Risk Management

Of all benefits of sustainability, one of the greatest is the long-term view of benefits and threats. This encourages due diligence via:

- Feasibility studies

- Better monitoring

- Auditing and assessments

- Early involvement of stakeholders and collaboration throughout the project

- Innovative, strategic and whole-life thinking.

As such, the sustainable approach becomes a powerful tool to manage risks in a project or company. The discipline and efficiency it imposes, with the involvement of stakeholders at an early stage of the project, ensures nasty surprises are kept to a minimum. The innovative approach to finding new solutions, as well as the typical demonstration of good conduct, ensures quality and long-term financial savings - more so than other, more traditional approaches.

Sustainability as a Demonstration of Best Practice

Sustainability is also a fantastic way of demonstrating when things are done properly, especially in countries where sustainability is not mandated and there is no obvious driver. It offers proof of transparency and quality that's otherwise hard to demonstrate in more questionable business scenarios. In my chat with Pantelis Levantis, he highlighted how certifying a building via an official independent institution is often, in Greece, the only way to ensure best practice during the design and construction stages.

Risk Mitigation of Long-Term Investments

It's clear the wind is turning, since traditional investors have begun realising that the social and environmental performance of their assets is directly affecting the financial performance of their investments. That's especially relevant when their investments are long-term. It's not that investors have woken up all of a sudden to the screams of Extinction Rebellion protesters, but rather that they're concerned about the risks inherent to their portfolios, including environmental risks.

Between 2015 and 2020, companies with strong Environmental Social and Governance (ESG) practices have fared better in both the U.K. and the U.S. stock markets. In part, this may be due to superior financial performance. However, when researchers from the University of Hamburg conducted a meta-analysis based on 2,200 empirical studies released since the 1970s, they concluded that the business case for ESG investing was "empirically well-founded". Of the studies analysed, around 90% suggest a positive relationship between ESG factors and corporate financial performance (CFP). "Investing in ESG pays financially… the positive ESG impact on CFP is stable over time" the authors conclude. Research also suggests that – on some level – investors believe companies with better performance on ESG measures merit higher valuations.[40]

Risk management should be of interest to everyone involved. However, this can be a winning factor, especially with people who have a long-term interest in the project, like property portfolio owners and owners-occupiers, as well as those with direct responsibilities and accountabilities in a project, such as the main contractor or designers.

---

40 www.moneyweek.com/481615/sri-esg-how-ethical-and-sustainable-investing-went-mainstream/

Supply Chain Risk Mitigation

With companies relying on supply chains scattered around the globe, climate change, loss of biodiversity, poor labour practices, and resource depletion pose a huge risk to supply chains - and, in turn, to the companies that utilise them. Sustainability ensures the reliability and quality of supply, as well as ethical trading.

Unlike traditional forms of business risk, social and environmental risks manifest themselves over a longer period of time, affect the business on many dimensions, and sit largely outside the organisation's control. Remember the example of Innocent Drinks, implementing organic and sustainable solutions for their mango plantations in India? That move was key to ensuring better quality and a reliable supply of an essential ingredient in their products, which was otherwise affected by climate change. For Innocent, this entailed managing risks by making investment decisions and developing adaptive strategies *today*, so they could realise longer-term benefits and ensure business survival.

Therefore, sustainable procurement and thoughtfully chosen supply chains are key in ensuring the project hits its own sustainability targets and continues to operate.

Protecting a Company's Reputation with Sustainability

"A good reputation is more valuable than money."
-Publilius Syrus

Sustainability provides resilience to the products and companies involved; it future-proofs, protects reputation, and safeguards brand longevity.

Patagonia is a sterling example of a company that began a sustainability journey in an unexpected way. In 1988, they had to address health issues among their first store's employees: many showed respiratory problems due to formaldehyde and pesticides in the cotton garments stocked in the basement. Patagonia went organic in 1996. From there, they began scrutinising every aspect of their production chain, looking for more sustainable methods of doing business. Customers started to expect this ethical behaviour from them, and it's now one of Patagonia's strongest selling points. They own a corporate identity that's responsible and reputable.

On the other hand, not acting in a sustainable, responsible manner can harm a company's reputation. In 2018, Burberry, the upmarket British fashion label, destroyed unsold clothes, accessories, and perfume worth £28.6m to prevent them being stolen or sold cheaply. Guess what? They wanted to protect their reputation, but having their name all over the media, being named and shamed for their wasteful habits, didn't do any good either.

Growth

Finally, we evaluate the growth of a company beyond its wealth. Sustainability makes it possible to grow a company's workforce and buy their loyalty; attract talents and a strong customer base; and act as a catalyst for innovative thinking.

Sustainability as a Market Differentiator

At this point in history, while we'd love sustainability to be the norm for everyone, it still provides some marketplace differentiation, especially in fields where it's a relatively new feature. Because of increasing market demand and tougher regulations, it provides an advantage over competition that doesn't implement sustainability in their practices. That includes attracting:

- Talent to companies that operate sustainably.

- In the case of universities, students. The younger generations are more focused on the environment than ever before, so they expect the institutions that provide their education to contribute.

- Tenants who, as increasingly conscious consumers, demand that their homes be healthy and efficient.

- Customers. As mentioned in the *Increased Revenue and Market Share* paragraph, consumers and especially Millennials are very conscious of their purchasing power. Demand for sustainable products and services has dramatically increased in recent years, and it shows no signs of slowing down any time soon.

A life-cycle cost approach helps companies see the big picture, and understand what's durable and cheaper for their customers in the long run. As in the case of Patagonia, a sustainable product may be more expensive at the outset to produce and manufacture, but it will last longer, require less maintenance, and demand fewer replacements, making it cheaper over its lifetime. Sustainability encourages that we invert the trend of "disposable in the name of cheap and fast convenience", and it's a synonym of quality. As such, companies that produce sustainably have a reputation advantage over those that don't.

Increased Employee Productivity and Reduced Staff Turnover - and, Therefore, Hiring and Severance Expenses.

The least appreciated element of sustainability is probably the human factor. It's been demonstrated by numerous studies that sustainability has a positive impact on the health and well-being of people, via better working conditions and healthier buildings. If you want more inspiration, take a look at the WELL standard, the certification scheme that rewards healthy buildings.

However, sustainability is not just about the 'making of stuff'. It's also present in the less tangible attitude of companies that nurture their employees, and it falls into the remit of Corporate Social Responsibility with issues such as equality, promotion of diversity, work/life balance, and reduction of pay gap. The 2018 Global Talent Trends study by Mercer[41] identified three factors that employees and job candidates are seeking in a company. This included permanent workplace flexibility, a commitment to health and well-being, and working with a purpose.

A company's staff are its biggest asset and liability at the same time. Treating them well, by ensuring all their needs are fulfilled, will repay a company in loyalty, staff retention, and productivity.

---

41   The study took a multi-perspective approach and collected input from 800 business executives and 1,800 HR leaders, as well as 5,000-plus employees across 21 industries and 44 countries around the world. www.mercer.com/our-thinking/career/global-talent-hr-trends.html

Employees leave a company for a variety of reasons. Aside from below-average compensation or horrible bosses, they also leave because of a cultural incompatibility or an unhealthy work environment, which sustainability can help with. Unhappy employees lead to poor business performance, absenteeism, negative company image, toxic team dynamics, reduced productivity, and disrupted continuity of business operations. The way businesses treat their employees can make or break the company.

A sustainable building, furthermore, shouldn't be underestimated. A healthier environment translates into reduced absence for sickness and better staff retention. These can be considerable savings, since, on average, a company spends 1% of their revenues in energy, 9% in rent, and 90% in staff-related costs.[42]

There are fascinating studies on how patients in hospital have 8.5% shorter stays, when they have access to outside views. In day-lit buildings, productivity is increased by 18%, students learn up to 26% faster, and retail sales increase by up to 40%.

Studies that have shown that 10% of employee absence can be attributed to working in environments with no connection to nature. That connection with nature reduces absenteeism by 15%, while also increasing mental function by up to 25%.

Take a look at Maslow's pyramid of needs, and suggest to your clients that they must, at least, have the physiological and safety needs of their employees as an absolute priority. The higher up the pyramid the company pushes its ethos, the better their employees will feel and the more benefits the company will reap.

How Sustainability Leads to Innovation

"The more a person limits himself, the more resourceful he becomes."
-Soren Kierkegaard, philosopher

---

42   www.ukgbc.org/ukgbc-work/health-wellbeing-productivity-offices-next-chapter-green-building/

Sustainability often equals innovation, because of the push towards creating unconventional solutions to old problems, within the constraints imposed by the discipline it requires. These constraints may be the use of certain materials, or the drive for low or zero energy, carbon, and water, etc.

In construction, various constraints imposed by sustainability frameworks are an excellent method of stimulating alternative and creative thinking. In the Living Building Challenge, for example, materials mustn't contain any harmful chemicals featured in the Red List; that motivates designers to find alternative, innovative solutions.

In fact, this is how sustainability frameworks (like LBC, but also **BREEAM**, **LEED**, Green Star, and all the others) should be viewed: as a springboard to push the designers to find innovative solutions. Sometimes this means finding the root of issues, eliminating them there, and then choosing the simplest fix, often borrowed from the past and from whatever is at hand locally.

Nike embedded sustainability and created the $1 billion-plus Flyknit line, which uses a specialised yarn system that requires minimal labour and generates large profit margins. Flyknit reduces waste by 80% when compared with regular cut-and-sew footwear. Since its launch in 2012, Flyknit has reduced 3.5 million pounds of waste and fully transitioned from yarn to recycled polyester, diverting 182 million bottles from landfills.

Joining the Dots of the Business Case for Sustainability

You now have all the elements to go out and sell sustainability to your clients.

Put together a strategy on how to approach a new client. You can use the checklist in the Action Steps Workbook to guide you.

The most important part is: do it. Be playful about it. All new skills require time to develop and become second-nature, so try the techniques I suggest, but also be curious. Step outside your comfort zone! That's where the excitement begins.

Building the Matrix

You can develop a matrix of benefits relevant to your client (on a personal level and at the company level, where relevant) using the tables in the Action Steps Workbook.

You can see a summary of them below.

You can also use the Influencing Strategy crib sheet available on the Green Gorilla website[43] to create a full business case for your client, taking into account their personality, sustainability maturity level, and drivers.

Financial / ROI benefits

- Obtain licence to operate (e.g. regulations; client's own policies or contract).

- Reduce upfront investment costs (via designing waste out, materials efficiency, optimised transport, lean processes, etc.).

- Sell/rent more quickly (e.g. real estate assets).

- Sell at a premium.

- Increase employee productivity.

- Reduce absenteeism.

- Reduce operational and maintenance costs (via energy and water savings).

- Reduce cost / frequency of component replacements over time.

- Increase longevity of product/asset.

- Access finance (green bonds, investments, government incentives).

---

43 www.thegreengorilla.co.uk/sustainable-the-book

Risk Management Benefits

- Encourage due diligence.

- Comply with CSR obligations.

- Increase resilience of product/asset/company.

- Avoid fines related to pollution, waste, or non-compliance with laws.

- Reduce risks connected to supply chain volatility.

- Minimise faults in the installation/assembly of components.

- Protect the company's brand and reputation.

- Manage company and projects better.

- Reduce complaints from customers/users.

- Improve performance.

Brand and Growth Benefits

- Gain an edge over the competition.

- Have a powerful marketing story in an increasingly competitive, demanding market.

- Innovate and produce original products/assets.

- Attract and retain customers.

- Make the brand and company resilient.

- Make the product/asset resilient.

- Encourage feedback loops and learning for future projects.

- Attract and retain talent.

- Access more bids/investments.

- Access new markets.

Key Points to Remember

Feel free to use this space for jotting down notes on your personal takeaways from this section.

CHAPTER 4 -

Resilience and Grit: Are These the Most Important Skills of All?

Buzzwords are a marketing obsession, as we know, and although the 'S' word (sustainability) might not always be one, in recent years I've often heard *"resilience"* as a substitute for it.

I don't personally believe that *sustainability* and *resilience* are synonymous. Resilience only looks at one aspect of sustainability (resist and recover from adversity), not at the impact a building, a product, or our behaviour has on the environment. Nonetheless, I do believe resilience, when applied to people, is an invaluable skill to develop.

This industry is ever changing, because it responds to dynamic macro-level challenges (like the 17 UN Sustainable Development Goals) that affect humanity as a whole, down to the city level, to the building level, to the lifestyle level, to the product level (food, clothes, materials, travel, and so on). From climate change to our decisions at the supermarket, from the macro to the micro level, every choice and every action is interconnected to others at other levels.

Every aspect of life and every one of our actions has an effect on the planet - and that's what sustainability looks at.

So if you've chosen to work in sustainability, it's no wonder you feel overwhelmed by the amount of information you need to acquire and keep up with: technical, political, economic, and cross-disciplinary.

Additionally, clients and other people that often don't share your sustainable heart need convincing. These are not believers that the Earth is flat, but the average, educated people, who still believe that sustainability is a frivolity, not a necessity.

Working in sustainability requires a deep passion for the subject and the end goal, which goes far beyond the need to pay your bills each month. That's why resilience is a key skill if you're in this profession, or are planning to join it.

The ability to bounce back will make you stronger in the long run and teach you how to deal with those setbacks the next time. The key is:

- Don't take it personally

- Find alternative ways to channel your anger and frustration

- Channel it until you've built a strong enough approach to influencing others and driving them towards your goals.

Then there's another skill, one that's earned great interest recently: *grit.*

Studied in depth and brought to the general public's attention by Angela Lee Duckworth[44], grit is the capacity to sustain interest and effort towards long-term goals. Grit is tenacity applied to your final vision.

Duckworth suggests that grit is a strong predictor of future success, more so than academic qualifications and IQ. Think for a second of Sir Richard Bran-

---

44   www.angeladuckworth.com/

son, a college dropout and dyslexic; judging by his academic outlook, the odds were against him. The man is now worth $4 billion and has started over 400 business ventures, as well as taken people to the Moon for leisure (I have to confess, I have his photo framed on my desk next to that of my parents, and I live by his motto, *"Screw It, Let's Do It"*). Branson might be not a sterling example of sustainability leadership - with his airline and cosmic travel aspirations - but he certainly embodies a strong personal success story.

I'm not suggesting that grit alone will make you a billionaire, but it will certainly make the goals you pick more attainable.

So how to develop your grit, or mental toughness?

Start by growing a new mindset, where setbacks and failures are viewed as both temporary and as opportunities to learn (as discussed in the *How to Overcome Your Fear of Failure* paragraph). This persistence will help you achieve meaning and fulfilment in your career - if you're strong enough to still be there - disappointment after disappointment.

Of course, only fools will bang their heads against the wall until they bleed. You should pause if challenges are so overwhelming that you feel ill, mentally or physically, or if you realise that, actually, this career isn't for you after all.

But if your professional goals are genuinely aligned with who you are as a person, then it's worth developing your resilience and grit. These traits will support you in the coming journey.

To do that, I suggest taking James Clear's three-step approach[45]:

Step:1

Define what grit (or mental toughness) means to you. It could be:

- Volunteering every Saturday at your local environmental charity.

- Waking up early every day to write a blog on sustainable living.

- Campaigning for action against climate change.

Ask yourself: what is your passion? Your ultimate goal?

---

45 www.jamesclear.com/grit

What does your heart truly desire, from a professional point of view?

For most of us in sustainability, it's making a difference and being rewarded for it. Our values drive our work; we develop our careers not just for the money, but to see the fruit of our hard work positively impact the environment, the people, and the planet for generations to come. It's not for the faint-hearted, but if this isn't a strong motivator, I'm not sure what is!

The other important element is to believe in yourself and in your capacity to reach these goals. As we've seen in the *Change the Way You See Yourself* paragraph, you can rewrite your mental book of limiting beliefs. You can change your brain by exercising it each day, no matter your current stage of life.

Step 2:

Build grit with small, tangible wins.

"Mental toughness is like a muscle. It needs to be worked to grow and develop", Clear says, and I couldn't agree more. Once your goal is established, it means showing up every day based on your commitment, not on the mood of the day.

How do you show up every day? It can't be just *once in a while*, when you land a new client or attend a big conference where the spirits are high. What everyday work will you contribute to reach your ultimate destination?

- Perhaps you'll commit to reading about your profession each morning during your commute, or attending one CPD webinar a month to keep up your technical knowledge.

- Maybe you'll commit to practicing assertiveness with your colleagues and clients at every opportunity.

- Maybe you'll better organise your work, so that every action is recorded correctly (as we'll discuss in the next chapter about *People and Project Management*).

- Maybe you'll advance your projects by starting on the toughest bit each day, even if that's unpleasant.

- Maybe you'll bounce back from a knock out, a bad meeting, or an argument with a commitment to improving and doing better next time. You can choose to ignore the inner critic that says, *"This happened because you're not worth it; you're an impostor."*

Step 3:

Build strong habits and stop depending on motivation.

*You don't have to be more courageous, more talented, or more intelligent —
just more consistent.*

That's truly what separates the professionals from the amateurs, in any path of life.

If you commit to taking one small action towards your goal and improve 1% every day, instead of contributing one giant effort now and then, you will be 365% better in a year's time.

Sustainability professionals have one big advantage: we have a higher purpose, and values to support our motivation along the way. Having an interest in something is generally not enough to move you towards excellence in your field every day. It's your higher purpose that offers this power. It's the willingness to align your end goal with your true self that can support you in waking up early, going to work via bike instead of car, reading your industry magazine, or studying for a self-improvement course during your lunch hour instead of scrolling social media.

Do you make the most of your time? If you sleep for eight hours and work for another eight, you have eight negotiable hours to play with every single day. How do you choose to spend those? It's entirely your choice.

When I commuted, at one point, I decided to leverage that time. It was a hell of a commute, with a journey of two and a half hours each way, which I endured for three years. I could have sunk and cried, played video games, or spent all my time on Facebook. Instead, I decided to study for my MSc, I meditated, I read book after book, I wrote, sometimes I slept (you need to cut yourself some slack now and then, and rest is an important part of your success). Five hours of my day were spent in a train carriage, and I discovered how to make those five hours count.

Try to evaluate your day for little pockets of spare time - even if it's just 30 minutes - where you can work on your goal. Remember, it's the turtle that wins, not the hare.

Key Points to Remember

Feel free to use this space for jotting down notes on your personal takeaways from this section.

CHAPTER 5:

People and Project Management

Nuggets of Project Management Applied to Sustainability

If you're a sustainability professional - especially a consultant - chances are, you'll find yourself dealing with your client, a budget, projects that have specific timeframes, a project team to coordinate – often not *your* team, so people who don't report to you - documentation to produce and coordinate, and other bits and bobs along the way.

Like it or not, whether you've received formal training before this point or are flying blind, you are a project manager. The trouble starts when someone who lacks any formal training in project management is required to coordinate various elements as just described as an external consultant, so without formal authority over anyone supposedly working for you; within budget and a timeframe dictated by the client, not by the actual amount of work required to deliver it; and you're expected to deliver as per the standard required by the client.

www.projectcartoon.com/

I love this classic, customisable tree-swing cartoon, joking about how subjective the perception of a project can be, depending on who is looking at it. But that's not all: the client probably needed something very simple and very different from what they described - and definitely from what was delivered - and the good project manager knows that. A good project manager (just like a good sustainability professional) can listen and ask the right questions to uncover the heart of their clients' needs - and then deliver in line with those needs, sometimes in contrast to their wants (remember the story of the child asking for chips on the seashore?).

When I worked at the BRE Innovation Park as Business Development and Account Manager, I realised I was a project manager without the qualifications.

I found myself winging it, without a real understanding of what I was supposed to do or of how complex projects worked. So, I asked my boss to send me where I could learn the skills. Shortly after, I was in a five-day, full-immersion project management training course.

I've been through the pain, so let me share some project management essentials that you need to be aware of as a sustainability professional. Of course, if you're required to coordinate projects or even programmes with numerous sub-projects, you should really consider attending a course yourself - but this should get you started.

The Aim of a Project Manager

Let's start with the aim. You could argue that the most important aim of project management is to deliver to the client's expectations. Certainly, that's an element of that – but, as mentioned before, part of your due diligence is to ensure what they require is *actually* what they need.

You're there to ensure the project stays within the limits of budget, time, and quality, which are terms established right at the beginning of any project. That means *managing risks;* and when I say risks, I include both negative, unforeseen circumstances *and* positive opportunities that manifest along the way.

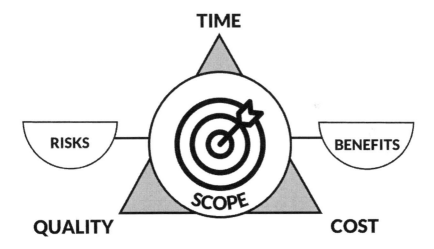

What key factor distinguishes project management from just "management"? The former has a final deliverable and a finite timespan, unlike organisational management, which is an ongoing process. It's a delicate balance to achieve the planned objectives in accordance with an agreed timescale, a fixed budget, and the client's acceptance criteria (the minimum quality required - as an example, if you deal with environmental assessments, that would be your target rating).

In this process, unexpected issues may arise, positive or negative. A classic one is a change in budget, which tends to be budget miscalculations or unexpected cuts, but can also be (far less often) extra funds released, perhaps from savings due to using automation or from lifecycle costing calculations.

The aim of the project manager is to ensure the project is delivered in spite of these unexpected changes, while keeping the budget–quality–time triangle as balanced as possible.

Now, managing a process with a (hopefully) sustainable outcome means accounting for certain extra factors:

- First of all, a project only exists when a beginning and end are defined.

  Sustainability, however, has an inherent long-term breath that, although technically stretching outside a project's timeline, will need to be taken into consideration. You can't manage a project with sustainability as a desired outcome without looking at the long-term impact of the project on the environment and people. You should also understand the company's long-term aspirations and vision, so you can align the project with them.

- For an outcome to be sustainable, a project can't be measured purely on functional quality. "Quality" is measured as the capacity of the final product to perform satisfactorily and in line with its intended purpose. In a sustainable project, quality must also be measured in terms of its social and environmental impacts, as well as its ability to enhance the life of people and the environment. This implies added consideration on procurement, choice of suppliers, ethical labour, impact on communities, resilience, environmental impact of materials and processes, compliance with standards, and best practice guidance.

- When evaluating the costs of a sustainable product, its entire lifecycle should be considered. Alongside the realisation costs, the project team should estimate the costs on its future users when the project is over (for example, the cost of maintenance, part replacements, and operation).

- You should account for the uniqueness of your position. Coordination and project management may be an incidental responsibility for you, whilst your role will probably be focused on advising or designing solutions for the project.

I often think of the fine balance between time, budget, and quality as the game *Operation!* There, you perform surgery on a scared chap with a red, light-up nose and remove his bones with tweezers - all without touching the metal edges of the little slots where the bones fit, or else you'll activate the buzzer.

Project managers must reach the end of the game without setting off the buzzer. You don't have to be Superman and over-deliver to finish the job properly. In fact, you *simply* need to keep within the boundaries of time, budget, and quality.

But, of course, simple does not mean easy.

The Tottenham Football Stadium was scheduled for completion in September of 2018. Not only did the works drag on for an extra six months, but the costs more than doubled, from £400 million to £875 million.

During the works, the stadium ended up in the news for all the wrong reasons: fire safety risks, wiring issues, electrical contractors re-doing their work three times because of clashes in scheduling with the HVAC contractors, even site workforces on drugs. This shambolic outlook appeared to be thanks to the main contractor lacking a project manager role. The subcontractors dealt directly with the football club, rather than answering to the main contractor, and that may have contributed to the whole mess.

As an extreme case of leaving good project management by the wayside, it perfectly illustrates how important this role is.

Nowadays, shouldn't a mature industry like construction be well-aware of the value of good project management? Well, as illustrated by the tree cartoon and the Tottenham Stadium example, there are certain factors always present in any project. They can dramatically affect the results and should be on a good project manager's radar.

They can be condensed into three: people, technology, and process.

People

Wouldn't it be great if we didn't have to deal with people? Of course it's a joke, I'm not a misanthropist, but it's true: when managing a project, people can profoundly affect the way it's accomplished.

To ensure a project runs smoothly, you must understand the needs of the team. This can be difficult. The client may not know what they want - and worse yet, the rest of the team may have different perceptions of what's necessary for the project. To handle this, revisit the initial chapters on listening to ensure you understand all your stakeholders' needs exactly. Most importantly, put everything in writing to avoid misunderstandings.

Your next issue is if you're called to deal with sustainability as an outside figure; despite being the expert, you'll have no direct control or authority over the project team. That means guiding decisions indirectly. By now, you should have the tools to influence others even if you're not their boss. If needed, revisit the chapter discussing influencing techniques.

As the PM, you're also responsible for ensuring all members of the wider team are clear on their role in the project. You may be familiar with the RAS-CI matrix. Try using a simple matrix to establish:

- Who is *Responsible?*

- Who is *Accountable?*

- Who is *Supporting* with man-hours or information?

- Who needs to be *Consulted?*

- Who should be kept *Informed?*

Often, projects unravel because responsibilities aren't clearly outlined. With sustainability in particular, if you're the sustainability consultant, your client may think you're actually responsible and accountable for "all things sustainability". However, you'll rarely finish your contracted work without the help of a wider team, even if that just involves providing you with access to information or specialist expertise.

Sustainability requires a big collaborative effort.

Because it's all-encompassing and covers everything from technology, to policies and behaviours, to people, any project with sustainability as an objective needs the whole team's approval and support.

If you hope to deconstruct the barriers of silo mentality when working in projects, a very effective approach is the Integrated Design Process. Although designed specifically for the British Columbia Green Building Roundtable as a building-related tool, nothing stops you from borrowing its principles and applying them to your industry, whether that's manufacturing, fashion, food, or anywhere else sustainability can be applied.

The key principles of the IDP are:

*   *High performance outcome.* The goal is to obtain a quality product/process at the end of a project, and clearly define how quality is measured via environmental certification or, for example, via a measured reduction of CO_2, energy, water, waste etc. when compared to a baseline.

*   *Well-defined environmental and social goals.* How is this project and its goals improving the environment, and how are people benefiting from it? Is the supply chain ethically sound? In good project management fashion, it's important that objectives are SMART (specific, measurable, attainable, realistic, and time-bound). Therefore, absolute clarity and communication are key to reaching your objectives.

*   *Keeping within constraints of budget and schedule.* Sounds obvious, but it isn't always. It's very important to keep budgets and schedules tightly in check, because when the unexpected happens and a budget gets tighter, the sustainability ambitions of a project are often the first cut out of the picture.

*   *Multidisciplinary and collaborative team,* whose members make decisions together based on a shared vision and a holistic understanding of the project. This is the most fundamental aspect of the IDP, and the key for success in any sustainability process. An integrated team makes a project multi-dimensional, and if properly coordinated, ensures that risks are better managed. All the team members will have an overview

of the project's objectives and constraints from the beginning, and this can prevent costly mistakes later on.

• *Iterative process.* Throughout the project's lifetime, from inception to completion and operation, the whole team receives and provides feedback on a regular basis (the so-called 'feedback loop') to ensure adjustments can be made at any stage, before it's too late. This is also helpful in preventing mistakes in future projects. Regular check-ins with the team are not a sign of micromanagement, but an opportunity to keep sustainability high on the agenda and to offer support to the team, instead of giving them an assignment and disappearing for three months.

• *Different each time, not predetermined.* There is no such a thing as one-size-fits-all. Every project will likely have its own client, team, budget, constraints, location, regulations, etc. - and all of these will, consequently, create new variables in how the project evolves. Maintaining a flexible attitude and working to understand these variables will create space for innovation and help ensure each project is successful.

As you can see, these principles can be applied to any project in any industry. The key is, of course, collaboration. The IDP is heavily reliant on teamwork from the start, where the majority of the work is ensuring each member can add value to the project and has been consulted to avoid nasty surprises down the line.

As a PM, it's your responsibility to identify who the key players are, who must be involved, and who's kept in the loop throughout.

When the Team Doesn't Have Sustainability as a Priority

Another common issue is when a team's priorities do not align with your priorities. Sustainability is often perceived as an add-on, not a key objective of the project. As such, people will be tugged in every direction to handle their day-to-day workloads, and you'll need to fit this aspect of the project within their to-do lists. That's often one of the major frustrations for sustainability professionals.

But how can you overcome this issue? How can you re-write other people's priority lists?

You'll need to influence others, and make it clear *what's in it for them.*

Why should they do it?

As we've seen in the Best Influencing Techniques chapter, there are several ways to influence others depending on our audience and what we believe they're receptive to. This can include:

- An inspiring vision ("Imagine how you'll be remembered, as the first architect that built a cathedral entirely in bamboo!").

- Logic and reasoning ("This is part of what the local authority requires us to do and, unfortunately, without a sustainability appraisal, they won't grant us a building permit. But think about it, it's going to be great for your reputation, too!").

- Scaring them with the consequences ("Clients we had in the past made the mistake of not carrying out the pre-demolition audition as suggested. They ended up being sued and paying huge fines for not delivering on the sustainability objectives. This jeopardised their business.").

And so on.

Once you have the team on your side, committed to work with you on the sustainability aspects of the project, you need to make their lives easier. Otherwise, you may not get what you need from them. Remember, their plate is already full.

The best method is to automate this as much as possible for them. Create templates and checklists that can be used again and again. Don't let people reinvent the wheel every time. If you're carrying out an environmental assessment, you'll find specific trackers and project management tools designed to keep everyone in the loop, as well as make their contribution as speedy and painless as possible. However, you can always come up with your own.

It's also smart to anonymise some of the material created in previous jobs. If it's good quality, you can put it together in a portfolio of examples to show your future clients. That way, you have fewer chances for misunderstandings and misalignment.

Why Do People Resist Change and What Can You Do About It?

A common issue with people is their resistance to change.

It's a human reaction to resist change as a form of self-protection. Your challenge, however, is pushing new ways of thinking into a market that's, over the years, developed an established way of operating.

Some clients understand that they need to change their operations in order to accommodate sustainability.

As part of the research for this book, I spoke to Nicola Hogan, Space, Environment & Sustainability Officer at Goldsmiths University in London. The biggest frustration in her job was a lack of engagement from the student community about sustainable actions, and their resistance to change.

The university goes through 400,000 disposable cups a year. She noticed that students do not generally use reusable cups. Whilst no survey has been officially conducted to explain why, Nicola speculates it's because of convenience: they don't want to carry a reusable cup everywhere. Surprisingly, she found that environmental concerns are stronger amongst people in their 40s (senior staff and mature students), who combine these concerns with costs - two strong reasons for them to refuse a disposable cup.

If your clients display a similar resistance to change, it's worth trying to align their existing operations with sustainability. That way, the switch is less traumatic and involves less effort.

To accomplish this, you need to thoroughly investigate the project and the project team's modus operandi, so you can align your priorities with theirs. It's a bespoke, crafted art that you need to fine tune, but the bottom line is:

Until sustainability becomes a no-brainer, so easy to implement that it's the obvious choice, we'll all struggle to push this agenda to the masses.

So the question you have to ask yourself is: how can I make this easy / convenient / obvious / appealing to my client?

For example,

- You can provide templates.

- You can check in with them every week.

- You can look for elements in their project that are simple like-for-like swaps.

- You can assign responsibilities and circulate an updated project plan every week, with outstanding and completed tasks.

- You can identify "champions" within the team who are more motivated than others and, crucially, have authority or are popular. They will advocate your business case for sustainability and advance the project more quickly.

- You can celebrate each success and progress with the team to boost morale.

The key is to understand how you can *help them* to *help you.*

Perception of Pessimism

Regarding the "people" factor, a classic difficulty in project management is the so-called *perception of pessimism.* Often, sustainability professionals and project managers arrive into a project as external consultants; effectively strangers in these people's lives, here to disrupt the way they've always worked. Obviously, the first reaction from the team is resistance; you aren't seen favourably and might encounter immediate opposition.

Human nature can easily create mistrust towards people who aren't part of the tribe. As such, the only solution is to quickly win over the team. Forget the iron fist (although it might be necessary when things get tough, or when you don't have the luxury of time). In general, exercising your empathy muscle will pay back in trust and collaboration - two fundamental aspects for any environmental project's success.

- Try to understand their concerns.

- Show the new team that you're on their side.

- ◆ Outline what's in it for them, as described above.

- ◆ Make it clear that you understand their point of view.

- ◆ Show that you're addressing their concerns as best you can. You're there to support their best interest, not disrupt their lives.

This should help integrate you as part of the team quickly.

Technology

When approaching a new job with your project manager's hat on, you'll see how any new project implies risks connected to technology.

Working processes and methods go through cycles of evolution. If the industry you're working on is anything like construction, then you know how it's risk-averse and generally reliant on traditional methods. Sustainability, on the other hand, pushes the envelope and always seeks new methods of delivering quality and long-term value - with less energy, carbon, and waste. So the clash is evident.

As the project manager, it's your role to understand the risks and opportunities in new technologies or methodologies. You're also responsible for establishing measures to limit the risks, as well as reassure your stakeholders that everything has been addressed.

How do you accomplish that? A good approach is to carry out your due diligence. If you suggest any new technology or methodology, or the team is planning to implement it, you must understand where (and if) it's been employed before and with what outcome. Modelling before implementation is a time and money saver. Any change should be put to the test on a computer before it's implemented in your project. Even a classic SWOT (strengths, weaknesses, opportunities, and threats) analysis can help understand whether a certain solution is the right one for the project.

Moreover, when adopting new methods, you must ensure the team has enough competent members to implement it in the safest, most effective way. For anyone who lacks the correct knowledge, adequate training must be provided. In sustainability (and especially in construction), one huge aspect of concern is the fallout of incorrectly implementing new technology - from design to installation to use. If any stage is not handled correctly, chances are, the technology will either gather dust and not fulfil its intended purpose, or even cause damage, like increasing emissions and negatively impacting the environment.

Remember my university client, who bought a massive, red biomass boiler that was never used? That's a classic example of a well-intended effort to save emissions ending up as a huge waste.

Processes

Finally, if you act as a project manager in your next job, be aware of the governance processes surrounding the project team you work with. You may find yourself dealing with bureaucracy and red tape, including the time needed for the approval process within your client's organisation. Likewise, you might experience frustration with the regulatory bodies, the certification body's quality assurance, and other approval bodies.

On the other hand, some organisations have a total lack of control and structure. Have you ever worked with a team that just went with the flow, perhaps working on smaller jobs that didn't have a set process? In this case, you should establish a *gateway system* for approval, meaning you agree with the team that the project cannot progress unless all the sustainability milestones have been achieved.

Some environmental work is very time-sensitive - like considering the location or procurement route - and that gives a certain degree of structure and action-traceability needed to obtain results. In any case, it's important to finish all the necessary steps in one given stage before moving on to the next. This will ensure the successful completion of your project - and give you some peace of mind.

Let me tell you something that sounds utterly trivial: a structured approach is the key to successful project management. I know, you think I'm stating the obvious.

But have you dealt with an organisation where the hot potato is passed on from one manager to the next? Where deadlines are missed every single time? Where documentation is lost and effort is duplicated?

I have, and it's not pretty. You have to do someone else's job because they seem incapable of doing it themselves - or they haven't got the time; there isn't a proper accountability structure in place when people would rather scroll through social media than do what they're paid for; there isn't a simple and clear system of gathering evidence; projects become unnecessarily complicated and the risks connected to them increase exponentially. Remember the football stadium example? You don't want to end up there.

For that reason, when starting a new project, it's worth:

1. Spending some time understanding its context. Use the PESTLE (Political, Economic, Social, Technological, Legal, Environmental/Ethical) model, as illustrated in the *Selling 101* chapter.

2. Identifying all the risks and opportunities connected to the actual project. Try to speak to as many people involved as possible, so you can look at it through the eyes of an insider. If you're thinking this is a waste of time, think again. A simple, half-hour brainstorming session with key people familiar with the project can do the trick, so long as you identify potential risks connected to people, technology, and process.

3. Thinking about the probability of these risks happening, then putting measures in place to avoid unforeseen and unwanted consequences.

4. Reviewing your risk management plan every so often, and definitely when one of the key factors – people, technology or process – change.

How Can you Accelerate Your Success as a Project Manager?

So far, I talked about avoiding potential risks and managing unwanted issues.

How about putting your successful sustainability professional hat on, and see how you can accelerate your success in any project you work on?

Last year, I was at a sector exhibition in London, where I attended an impressive talk. The guy speaking made headlines in our sustainable construction world by leading his team at Sweco to win "BREEAM Company of the Year" three times (in 2014, 2016, and 2017). He was personally awarded the "BREEAM Assessor of the Year" title in 2016. Beyond that, he secured the highest ever BREEAM score - 98.5% - on the Bloomberg HQ building in London, along with several other 'Outstanding' buildings after that.

I personally renamed him the Midas of Sustainability, because anything he touches turns into green gold. I grabbed the opportunity to speak with him at the end of his talk and invited him to be interviewed for the Green Gorilla Conversations series. What exactly is his magic formula for getting such sterling results?

Kartik Amrania is a delightfully humble man. He attributes this good fortune mainly to his team, but also to his engineering background, which allows him to find innovative solutions to old problems.

- In fact, that's one of three key elements in successful sustainability projects. In construction (and other fields, too), *innovation* allows you to respond creatively and find new solutions, where traditional methodologies and behaviours can't help.

  Fair enough, not everyone has Kartik's genius for new engineering solutions - but surely brainstorming with the team to find new ideas, feeding your curiosity by reading, going to sector conferences and exhibitions, asking questions, observing and trying to think outside the box, and questioning the 'set in stone' rules and practices can put you on the right path.

- Kartik's second ingredient is *life cycle assessments* (LCA). Evaluate the lifespan of your product/building/process, and look at the impact it will have over that time in economic, social, and environmental terms. If the balance is positive long-term, then you're on the right path to making your project truly sustainable. Often sustainability professionals fail to convince their clients to analyse their projects' lifetime, usually due to the cost of an LCA assessment. But this is a key element of success of any project. More so, why not challenge the status quo and see whether the product/project can be created as a circular economy product, which never ceases providing value and never ends up in landfill?

- Finally, Kartik's triad of key success elements in a sustainability project involves something I've stressed frequently in this book: *collaboration*.

"No man is an island" is even truer in sustainability, where every single member of the team needs to pull together towards a meaningful result.

Sustainability, I can't stress this enough, is not an overlay for the "business as usual" work. It needs to trickle down into every pore of a project; it needs to inform every decision; it needs to have every single stakeholder on board, from the client, to the project team, to the end user. It's the *new* business as usual.

To ensure the best results, it must have this beautiful orchestra of talented musicians playing together from the beginning, working in harmony throughout the song, and ending is a well-organised flourish. Sustainability can't be a mere afterthought.

The Importance of a Feedback Loop

Issues arise when a team fails to check up on a project after it's finished. How many clients actually keep an eye on the performance of their final product?

Some industries closely inspect how their products perform, such as with manufacturing companies. In construction, where the product is a building, that's rare. It's like throwing a message in a bottle out to sea, uncaring of where it ends up. All too often, project teams and clients don't want to know what happens when the project is over, because it ceases to be any of their concern. Foolish excuses (like, *"We don't have time"*, or, *"We don't have resources")* are all you'll get. Suddenly, the world is no different than when you started that project, if not a bit worse.

How deeply irresponsible.

Maintaining an interest in past projects may be the key to limiting future mistakes.

And although there is no easy fix to this issue, it's worth embedding in contracts that commissioning of the final product is carried out as a routine action, whenever possible. It's also worth asking the project team about the in-use performance of their past projects; this will highlight to them how important it is to learn from past experiences.

The Importance of Setting Systems for Productivity

Establish your Priorities

A priority system reduces ineffectiveness and saves time.

I realised that whilst working at **BRE** as a technical consultant and seeing the struggles of **BREEAM** assessors first-hand. They spent many hours trying to come up with a system to streamline a complex assessment process - one made of hundreds of elements, which didn't come in any particular logical or chronological order, aside from being grouped together by environmental issues.

How could I make the assessors' job easier and more productive? I had this idea of writing a book that would help sustainability consultants integrate sustainability (and **BREEAM** in particular, so it wasn't an afterthought) with the day-to-day running of a construction project.

The book was endorsed by the RIBA[46]. Although the final title was less than catchy – *Integrating BREEAM Throughout the Design Process* – it ended up a bestseller of the publisher in that first year.

I was mentored and supported in this project by a principal consultant and scientist, who had already written several digests and technical publications. In fact, she'd been one of the inventors of **BREEAM**: Dr. Josephine Prior.

In the book, I had a chance to thoroughly analyse the processes necessary for a construction project to be carried to completion, and then map that against the **BREEAM** process. At that stage, RIBA had published a new **RIBA** Plan of Works with a sustainability overlay, and it made sense to use that as a timeline and milestone reference - although, obviously, projects take various forms, including different procurement routes.

A vital lesson I gleaned from writing that book (which has been invaluable in writing this one) is the importance of setting a priority system. The **BREEAM** assessment is made of hundreds of different credits, all demanding the team's attention, and a good 30%-plus need to be implemented from the word "go".

---

46   Royal Institute of British Architects

I reckon this is a valid principle for your working life in general, not just for environmental assessments.

You might often find yourself mid-morning, faffing with your emails, getting distracted by the latest office gossip during a second coffee round, dealing with stuff that other people have dumped on your desk. Then, you suddenly wonder where the morning has gone. I guess you hadn't prioritised your time correctly. What if I told you that starting with a long to-do list and multitasking back and forth between those items doesn't make you any more productive?

Instead, use a roadmap that you can take to every project you accept, whether that's a BREEAM project or not, so that all your environmental goals are fulfilled, and your client is on board.

Rethink Your To Do List: the Ivy Lee Method

Have you heard of the Ivy Lee method?

James Clear[47] explains very well why this deceptively simple technique - created by productivity consultant Ivy Lee over one hundred years ago - is still very much worth its money today. Lee was paid the equivalent of $450,000 in today's money by his client, Charles M. Schwab, to implement this idea in his company.

The method consists of writing a to-do list no longer than six items every night, before going to bed. Order the items by their priority. As such, the first item you tackle in the morning is not reading your emails (unless your job depends on it that particular day), but accomplishing the first, most important task, and nothing else.

No multitasking. Close all your browser windows. Close your emails. Focus on that one thing and get it done.

---

47 www.jamesclear.com/ivy-lee

If you have trouble focusing on one thing only, try the Pomodoro Technique[48], another incredibly simple and effective way of managing your time. It works by laser-focusing your attention on one thing only for 25 minutes an instance. Then take a short break before starting with your next 25 minute 'pomodoro' stretch. Take a longer break after four pomodoros, until you've completed your task. You can download various Pomodoro Timer apps for free from the web - or use your kitchen timer!

Once the first priority task is done, cross it from the list you've created, then move on to the next priority, and so on. Anything left unfinished goes to the following day's to-do list. The advantage? You know in advance what you'll do each day, so you're prepared to crack on as soon as you sit down to work. You can be sure you're making real progress by tackling your most productive tasks first.

Aim to accomplish one or two very important things every day, and you're set for success. That's five to ten very important things in a week. All of a sudden, this method doesn't seem so trivial, right?

Apply the Ivy Lee Method to Sustainability

Break your project down into broad, *must-have* priorities. They can be dictated by your client, regulations, local authorities, or any other superior force you need to respond to. They may or may not be time-bound (although when tasks lack a deadline, they tend to be ignored or delayed. A little piece of advice: give yourself a deadline even if you don't have to).

What are key goals of this project that *must* be achieved? Is it finishing before Christmas? Building your product with no plastic whatsoever? If you're carrying out a BREEAM or LEED assessment, is it obtaining a specific certification rating?

---

48 Entrepreneur Francesco Cirillo created the Pomodoro Technique, now a renowned time-management tool used by millions of people all over the world, while a university student looking for a way to get more done in less time. He called it Pomodoro Technique after the tomato-shaped kitchen timer he initially used to keep track of his time. www.francescocirillo.com/pages/pomodoro-technique

Next, you should break down these goals into sub-priorities and actions, which serve as a strategy for reaching those goals within the set time and budget limits.

Using the BREEAM example, it could involve establishing set systems and responsibilities, then targeting the 'minimum standards' first, which are credit points that must be obtained for any certification rating to be achieved.

If you're investigating how to make your product completely plastic-free, then this first priority is to perform research and due diligence regarding other products on the market. Which claim to be plastic-free? Once you know what you're dealing with, you can spot a gap in the market. After that, you can investigate potential partners or consider investing in research and development.

Look at this second priority list; you can still break it down into top priorities and smaller actions. In BREEAM, look at the individual, 'minimum standard' credits you need to target, and explore the requirements for each. Who should be responsible for them? Assign those responsibilities to appropriate members of the team. In the product example, you could talk to manufacturers to explore alternatives to the plastic components, along with their prices and production timings.

You get the gist.

Five to six small, attainable tasks set day by day, without taking your eyes off the big picture, will earn you that big picture quickly.

You will have a greater chance of success by transforming these tasks into actionable items. Start them with a verb: *call* the engineer; *research* any constraints on the local authority website; *read* the latest sustainability report, etc. That way, in the morning, it will be crystal clear what you need to do, cutting down unnecessary time and decision fatigue. Make your tasks small enough that they don't seem daunting (I suggest 30 minutes or less), or else you will procrastinate.

You need to essentially fool your brain into action, by making the tasks accessible and easy to implement.

This isn't about (or only about) downloading the latest app that promises to make your life easier - although those apps have a place in the world and can truly help optimise your time.

I'm talking using your brain, a pencil, and a piece of paper to create systems, priorities, and actions that make sense to you. Then maybe use the app to streamline or keep you on track with automated reminders.

The Brain Dump method

If you feel overwhelmed at the beginning of a project - or even in the middle of it — use the Brain Dump method. On a piece of paper, dump all the stuff you have in mind and that you must do in connection to the project. This will have the additional psychological advantage of freeing your brain. Plus, you can immediately spot items that are irrelevant and not important.

Now start organising this list:

- Prioritise the important *and* urgent items first.

- Next will be important *but not urgent* items.

- Then, delegate them to others or cross them as not so important after all.

That's a classic method made famous by President Eisenhower, who reportedly used an importance vs. urgency table to prioritise his tasks. It's best known as the Priority Matrix:

	DO NOW	DO LATER
CRUCIAL	CRUCIAL - DO IT NOW!	CRUCIAL but you can do it later - PUT IN CALENDAR!
NOT CRUCIAL	NOT CRUCIAL but still urgent - DELEGATE	Why is this still in your 'TO DO' list?!

Once your priority items are established, transfer the top five or six to your daily to-do list.

The Pareto Principle

If you need more help checking your productivity levels, try applying the 80/20 Pareto principle to your work day. Ask yourself if you're spending 80% of your time on the most productive 20% of tasks (that's equal to your number-one and number-two items on the daily to-do list).

Project Management Systems and Tools

There are several project management tools that support collaboration and can make your life as a Project Manager easier. Certain digital systems will merely facilitate information-sharing (Google Drive, Office 365, Dropbox, Asana and Trello, just to name a few), whilst others will provide added structure to a project (like Prince2, Lean, Agile, or Critical Path Method (CPM)). These tools aim to maximise the use of resources and time, but they differ in complexity and focus. Your choice of framework will depend on a number of factors, such as the type of project, its complexity, and your experience.

Depending on how you work and the type of projects you accept, you may be familiar with several or have a favourite. I'm personally a huge fan of the humble Excel (and Google Sheets, because you can share and work simultaneously on a spreadsheet), since I can customise it as I please.

Gathering and Recording Evidence

In this type of work, it's very important to be hyper-systematic in how you collect and catalogue evidence. This is especially true when you have to seek certification, perform an environmental assessment, target an ISO certification, or perform anything else that will be audited. Receipts, certificates, letters, reports, and drawings can be the difference between achieving certification or losing it. As a project manager, it's your responsibility to carry out the job in the most efficient manner, and time is a crucial parameter to watch for. As an example, developing a naming system that clearly and uniquely identifies a document that's part of your evidence, from the thousands you may have in any single project, will save you grief and time before an audit.

Remember to add the project name or registration number, category and credit/point it refers to (if dealing with **BREEAM, LEED,** or **WELL**), dates, and version numbers as a minimum. Come up with a system that works in your company (for example, using a digital folder structure), that can be easily explained to anyone on the project, and that is simple to replicate.

Key Points to Remember

Feel free to use this space for jotting down notes on your personal takeaways from this section.

What Next?

Congratulations! You have reached the end of this book.

If you've followed my suggestions and practised the Action Steps, you're now in a better position to tackle your next meeting, project, or job. You feel more confident in your abilities, more capable of presenting before an audience, influencing others, selling them your sustainability ideas, and managing your project in an organised manner.

You feel empowered to reach your goals and to spread the sustainability message far and wide.

However, if you don't feel you're there yet, you want a little more help on your journey towards empowerment, or you want to find out more about the ideas covered in this book, visit www.thegreengorilla.co.uk. Here, you'll find more resources, our courses, and coaching options.

So, until next time:

Own your confidence.

Be curious.

Practise being a Green Gorilla.

This planet needs you.

Printed in Poland
by Amazon Fulfillment
Poland Sp. z o.o., Wrocław